Let Your Home Attract Love to You

For thousands of years, the Chinese have known that if they arrange their homes and possessions in the right way, they will attract positive energy into their life, including a life rich in love and friendship. Now you can take advantage of this ancient knowledge so you can attract the right partner to you; if you're currently in a relationship, you can strengthen the bond between you and your beloved.

It's amazingly simple and inexpensive. Want your partner to start listening to you? Display some yellow flowers in the "Ken" (communication) area of your home. Do you want to bring more friends of both sexes into your life? Place some green plants or candles in the "Chien" (friendship) area. To attract or recapture passion, bring touches of red into the "K'un" (feelings) area of your home. Red is the strongest and most stimulating of the colors, so be careful not to go overboard! Balance is the desired goal.

Feng Shui for Love & Romance will show you how to work with the universal forces of the heavens and earth—yin and yang energy, the five elements (Wood, Fire, Earth, Metal, and Water), and your love direction (East, West, North, or South)—to bring an abundance of love into your home and your life.

About the Author

Richard Webster was born in New Zealand in 1946, where he still resides. He travels widely every year, lecturing and conducting workshops on psychic subjects around the world. He has written many books, mainly on psychic subjects, and also writes monthly magazine columns.

Richard is married with three children. His family is very supportive of his occupation, but his oldest son, after watching his father's career, has decided to become an accountant.

To Write to the Author

If you wish to contact the author or would like more information about this book, please write to the author in care of Llewellyn Worldwide, and we will forward your request. Both the author and publisher appreciate hearing from you. Llewellyn Worldwide cannot guarantee that every letter written to the author can be answered, but all will be forwarded. Please write to:

Richard Webster
C/o Llewellyn Worldwide
P.O. Box 64383, Dept. K792-7
St. Paul, MN 55164-0383, U.S.A.

Please enclose a self-addressed, stamped envelope for reply, or $1.00 to cover costs. If outside the U.S.A., enclose international postal reply coupon.

FENG SHUI
for
Love &
Romance

RICHARD
WEBSTER

1999
Llewellyn Publications
St. Paul, Minnesota 55164-0383
U.S.A.

FIRST EDITION
First Printing, 1999

Book design: Amy Rost
Cover design: Tom Grewe
Interior illustrations: Jeannie Ferguson
Typesetting and editing: Michael Maupin

ISBN 1-56718-792-7 (pbk.)
Library of Congress Cataloging-in-Publication Data (Pending)
Webster, Richard, 1946–

Llewellyn Publications
A Division of Llewellyn Worldwide, Ltd.
P.O. Box 64383, Dept. K792-7
St. Paul, Minnesota 55164-0383

Printed in the United States of America

Other Books by Richard Webster

Feng Shui for Apartment Living

Feng Shui for the Workplace

101 Feng Shui Tips for the Home

Chinese Numerology

Astral Travel for Beginners

Spirit Guides & Angel Guardians

Aura Reading for Beginners

Seven Secrets to Success

Feng Shui for Beginners

Dowsing for Beginners

Numerology Magic

Omens, Oghams & Oracles

Revealing Hands

Forthcoming

in the Feng Shui series

Feng Shui in the Garden

Feng Shui for Success & Happiness

Dedication

For my friend Ed Rapoza, psychic, teacher, raconteur,
and wonderful host in Japan.

Acknowledgments

I would like to express my grateful thanks
to T'ai Lau for his help and advice.

Contents

Introduction

Feng shui is the ancient Chinese art of living in harmony with your environment. Thousands of years ago, the Chinese believed that if they arranged their homes and possessions in the right places, they would lead lives of contentment, abundance, and happiness. Obviously, this also included a strong, stable, loving and harmonious relationship, as without this we are unlikely to be contented and happy.

The sole purpose of this book is to help you make this a reality in your own life. Feng shui can help you attract and find the right partner, and it can also enable you to revitalize a current relationship. No matter who you are, you have a right to a rich, fulfilling relationship.

There are people who have no need for intimate relationships, but they are rare. Dr. James Lynch wrote: "all the available data points to the lack of human companionship, chronic loneliness, social isolation, and the sudden loss of a loved one as being among the leading causes of premature death in the United States."[1] Dr. Lynch concluded that loneliness could be related to almost every major disease, but was particularly evident in heart disease, which is the leading cause of death in the United States. "Millions of people," he wrote, "were dying, quite literally, of broken or lonely hearts."[2]

Researchers in different parts of the world have experienced similar results. Unquestionably, single, widowed, and divorced people die at a greater rate than people living in long-term relationships. Consequently, the people we love have a profound effect on our psychological well-being, and this in turn, has a dramatic effect on our physical health.

Loneliness has increased dramatically over the last hundred years, as people gravitate towards the cities. At the start of the twentieth century about eighty percent of the world's population lived in rural areas and knew all their neighbors. Now, one hundred years later, more than half of the world's population live in towns and cities, and it is common for apartment dwellers not to know the names of the people living next door.

I live in a city of just over one million people. At least a quarter of the homes in this city house only one person.[3] In fact, two out of every five adults in the Western world are single.[4] Many of these have been married, of course, but are now single again as a result of divorce, or the death of their partner. Some of these people have chosen to be single, and are happy with that decision. Others, though, become desperate for a partner, and this desperation increases in intensity as time goes on. Still others come from dysfunctional or abused backgrounds and cannot contemplate the thought of a permanent relationship.

In the past, people having problems with their sexual identities would often marry to try and resolve the problem.

Needless to say, this seldom worked and usually created pain and suffering for everyone involved. Fortunately, these people are likely to remain single nowadays, as they no longer feel obliged to marry to conceal their sexual orientation. Incidentally, everything in this book will work just as well for non-traditional relationships. Feng shui is totally non-discriminatory and is not limited to traditional relationships.

As you can see, there are many reasons why two out of every five adults are not living inside a permanent relationship. This is not to say that being single, or living on your own, is a bad thing. Many people find living on their own fulfilling and satisfying. Cliff Richard, the English pop singer, wrote: "I actually enjoy being single!"[5] In some ways, single people have the opportunity of being intimate with a much wider range of people than their friends who are married.

Human beings are social animals. We all need relationships with others to a greater or lesser extent. Friends and acquaintances can provide the help and emotional support we all need. Even a smile from a complete stranger we see on the street can provide enormous benefit as far as emotional health is concerned.

Naturally, a smile from your partner or close friend is even better. The greater emotional support, intimacy and nurturing that people inside a relationship receive from their partners has benefits far outweighing the obvious ones. For instance, a study in England showed that people who express their feelings to their partners are less likely to develop cancer.[6] Sociologists also discovered that working-class women who were able to discuss intimate matters with their husbands were less likely to suffer from depression at difficult times in their lives.[7]

There is also evidence to suggest that people who have children live longer than those who have none. This is despite the potential dangers of pregnancy and childbirth, and the fact that children invariably cause their parents a great deal of stress at different times.

However, if you are reading this, you do not need to be told any of the benefits of a loving, supportive relationship. I am assuming that you do not want to be on your own. I am also assuming that if you are already in a relationship, you want to do something to revitalize it and recapture the passion and intimacy that may have been lost.

This book is aimed at helping you achieve these goals. It begins with a brief look at the basic principles of feng shui. It then shows you how to use these ideas to attract the right love interest into your life. The five elements, which play an important part in feng shui, can also help you determine compatibility. These are examined to help you find the most compatible person for you. Finally, we look at improving existing relationships, and how to use feng shui to attract friends into our lives.

I hope that by studying this book and applying the simple principles, you will enjoy a rich, fulfilling relationship with someone who is both your lover and friend. Then you will be able to say, like the Shulamite bride in the *Song of Solomon:* "This is my beloved, and this is my friend."[8]

You have a right to a rich, full love life. This book will help you achieve it.

1

The Basic Principles

Feng shui has a history that goes back at least five thousand years. In China they have five mythical emperors who were responsible for ruling the country in prehistoric times. It is so long ago that no one knows if these mythical emperors ever existed. Each is credited with inventing something, and Wu, the very first emperor, is credited with discovering feng shui.

The legend goes that one day, while he and his men were doing irrigation work on the Yellow River, a giant tortoise crawled out of the river. This was considered an excellent omen, as in those days they believed that gods lived inside the shells of turtles and tortoises. However, when Wu looked more closely at the tortoise he found a perfect three-by-three magic square formed by the markings on the tortoise's shell. Each horizontal, vertical and diagonal row added up to fifteen.

$$\begin{array}{ccc} 4 & 9 & 2 \\ 3 & 5 & 7 \\ 8 & 1 & 6 \end{array}$$

This was considered so remarkable, that Wu called all his wise men to examine the tortoise. From their findings came, not only feng shui, but also the I Ching, Chinese astrology, and Chinese numerology. Even today, this magic square plays an extremely important role in feng shui.

Ch'i

Many thousands of years ago, the ancient Chinese discovered that if they built their homes in the right position, the quality of every part of their lives improved. The ideal position was a house that faced south, to receive the sun all day long, with hills behind to protect the home from the cold winds of the north. As well, there should be gently flowing water in front of the house (Figure 1A).

A home in this position would receive abundant *ch'i*. Ch'i is the universal life force that is found in all living things. It is created by anything beautiful in nature, such as a meandering stream, and in anything that is done perfectly. A skater performing a flawless routine is creating ch'i. Ch'i is nurtured by gently flowing water, and is carried along by gentle breezes. "Feng Shui" means "wind and water." This means slow, moving water and gentle, caressing breezes. Harsh, raging torrents of water, gales and hurricanes carry away all the good ch'i.

Figure 1A: Protected home

Shars

There is both positive and negative ch'i. Negative ch'i (usually known as *shar* ch'i) is created by straight lines or angles that are pointed directly at your home. They are particularly bad if they are aimed at your front door.

The worst form of shar is created when your house is situated on a T-junction, with a road heading directly towards you. It is interesting to note that Buckingham

Palace had this particular shar until the Queen Victoria memorial was built (Figure 1B).

Another common shar is created by the corner or roof-line of a neighboring house (Figure 1C). It is even possible to have shars on your own property. If the front entrance consists of a straight line heading directly towards your front door, it is a shar, sending "poison arrows" in your direction. A long internal hallway can also create a shar inside your home.

Fortunately, there is a remedy for virtually everything in feng shui.[1] The most effective way is to make the shar symbolically disappear. Consequently, a fence, hedge or trees could effectively conceal a straight road heading towards your property (Figure 1D). If you can not see it, it ceases to exist.

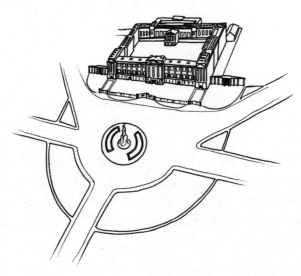

Figure 1B: The Queen Victoria memorial

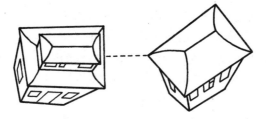

Figure 1C: Shar caused by roofline

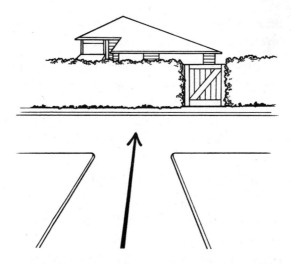

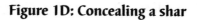

Figure 1D: Concealing a shar

It might not be possible to hide the shar in this way. In the East, when this occurs, they use a pa-kua mirror to send the shar back where it came from. This is an octagonal piece of wood, with a small circular mirror in the center. Around this mirror are placed the eight trigrams from the I Ching. This mirror is hung over the front door. The shar is then symbolically reflected back where it came from by the mirror. It is possible to buy pa-kua mirrors in novelty and import stores. These mirrors are extremely powerful and must never be used indoors.

The Nine Cures

In feng shui there are nine cures that can be used to remedy almost any feng shui problem (Figure 1E).

1. **Bright Objects:** Mirrors, lights and crystals, especially lead glass crystals, are examples.

2. **Living Objects:** Plants, flowers, ponds, and aquariums are good examples of this category. Artificial replicas also serve the same purpose. Consequently, artificial flowers, a ceramic animal, or a painting that depicts live animals and plants would also act as an effective remedy.

3. **Sounds:** Wind chimes and bells that make pleasing sounds in the breeze are good examples.

4. **Moving Objects:** Mobiles, fountains, and fans are examples of objects in this category.

5. **Heavy Objects:** Boulders, large stones, and statues are good examples.

6. **Hollow Objects:** Flutes and wind chimes are good examples. Incidentally, the tubes of wind chimes should always be hollow to allow the ch'i to rise inside them.

7. **Colors:** Colors, particularly when used in conjunction with the five elements, make useful remedies.

8. **Electrical Objects:** Stereos, radios, and televisions all create music that can be a useful remedy.

9. **Intuition:** We can sometimes be drawn to put a certain object in a particular place, without really knowing why. It pays to follow our intuition in this way, and use it to create effective remedies.

Figure 1E: The Nine Cures

Clutter

Removing clutter could almost be described as another remedy. Clutter has the effect of disrupting the smooth flow of ch'i through the house, which consequently causes problems. Many people are inclined to hoard things, just in case they need them again in the future.

Most people have items of clothing hanging in their wardrobes that they will never wear again. These items create clutter, and clearing them out can be extremely beneficial on a number of levels. It can indicate letting go of the past, something that is extremely necessary before embarking on a new relationship. It can indicate confidence in the future, as you demonstrate a belief that you will be able to buy more clothes as and when you need them. It can provide an incredible sense of freedom. Can you remember the feeling of release you experienced the last time you cleared out some junk?

Clutter can reveal itself in many different forms. For instance, if you deposit your clothes all over the floor when you go to bed at night, you are effectively cluttering up the room for the next eight hours.

Clutter restricts you and holds you back. If you are looking for a new relationship, you need to pay particular attention to the clutter in your home.

Figure 1F: Yin–Yang symbol

Yin and Yang

Everything in the universe can be divided into either yin or yang. You are probably familiar with the yin–yang symbol of two tadpole-like forms inside a circle (Figure 1F). Yin is black with a white dot, and yang is white with a black dot. The dot of yin inside yang, and the dot of yang inside yin indicates that there is always a small part of yin inside every piece of yang, and vice versa.

The yin-yang circle is the Taoist symbol of the universe and represents completion. Yin and yang were never defined. They represent the two opposites that can not live without the other. Front and back is an example. If there was no front, there could be no back. Night and day is another example. Without night, there could be no day. For the purposes of this book, male and female is probably the best example. Without one, there could not be the other.

Yin is passive, nourishing and nurturing. It represents the female principle.

Yang is aggressive, dominating and positive. It represents the male principle.

Yin and yang are continually striving for balance. There is constant tension between the two. At times, yang prevails and dominates yin, but then, as it starts to decline, yin takes over for a while. It is neither good nor bad when one takes precedence over the other: it just is. Neither is one better than the other when they are in equilibrium.

Flat land is described as being too yin, and mountainous terrain would be too yang. The best environment contains both, which is something the ancient Chinese knew all those thousands of years ago when they discovered the ideal location for a home.

Nowadays, of course, most of us live in cities and we have to use nearby houses to act symbolically as the protective hills behind our home.

A totally female environment would be considered too yin, just as an all male environment would be too yang. The best home, from a feng shui point of view, would contain just the right balance of yin and yang.

Yin and yang is really all about balance and harmony. We are all composed of a mixture of yin and yang energies. Naturally, women contain more yin than they do yang, and men more yang than yin. However, it is possible for a woman to express herself in a yang-like manner. Margaret Thatcher, the former prime minister of Great Britain, is almost revered in China because they see her as a "woman of yang."[2] In the same way, many men are passive and gentle, which means that they usually express themselves in a yin manner. However, as we are all comprised of both yin and yang, these passive men are also able to express the yang side of their natures when the situation demands it. The dot of yin inside the yang, and the dot of yang inside the yin clearly shows this. There is always a degree of the feminine inside the masculine, and a similar amount of masculine inside the feminine.

In real life, we have to look after both the yin and yang sides of our natures. A woman who is always passive, meek, mild, and giving, will quickly find herself being taken advantage of by almost everyone she meets. Likewise, a macho yang man who is constantly rude, aggressive, demanding, and self-centered will end up feeling isolated and lonely. We need to nurture and cherish both the yin and yang sides of our natures.

Health problems are often a sign that our balance of yin and yang has changed. Thousands of years ago, Chinese medicine divided everyone into the categories of yin (cool) and yang (hot). If someone is withdrawn, sluggish, tired and lacking in energy they are described as being too yin. Likewise, when someone is restless, agitated, high-strung, and nervy, he or she is said to be too yang. Chinese medicine looks at the whole body. Consequently, a cure for a headache might involve an acupuncture needle placed in the foot.[3]

Yin and yang is especially important for us as it denotes the relationships between women and men. Two of the hexagrams in the I Ching also exemplify this. Chien, the first of the sixty-four hexagrams, is comprised of six unbroken lines and is pure yang energy. Kun is made up of six broken lines, which represent pure yin energy. Both are positive images, but also denote a time of waiting, as they each lack the activating, nurturing power of the other.[4] There are many jokes and stories about how men and women are two totally different species and can never get on, but in reality, we need each other to lead complete, fulfilling lives.

In the I Ching, the male yang element is the aggressive, dominating, powerful one, while the female yin is weak, docile, and receptive. This goes back to Confucian and Taoist teachings which were male-dominated. Men ruled and women were subservient and obeyed their husband's commands. However, before the Shang dynasty began (about 1,500 B.C.E.) men and women were considered equal. The changes occurred gradually until the Taoists were teaching that women were evil people who drained men's vital energy, reduced his life span and prevented him from achieving immortality.[5]

Despite this, throughout history Chinese literature and art has portrayed a different picture where men and women are considered total equals and delight in each other's company. In fact, sexual intercourse was considered a spiritual union where women secreted yin essence and men yang.

In reality, most people lived their lives somewhere between these two extremes, and women were often second-class citizens. This allowed the men to achieve harmony and balance in their lives, but only as long as women remained passive and resigned to their roles.

This is why many of the old books seem extremely sexist to us today. However, they were written at a time when this was considered perfectly normal and was unquestioned by anyone. Yin and yang are always in a state of dynamic tension, and in the past, yang predominated over the yin. Today it is much more evenly balanced, but it is important to realize that if yin increases, yang decreases, and vice versa. This happens all the time in every relationship. There has to be give and take on both sides, and the yin-yang symbol clearly demonstrates this.

The Five Elements

The ancient Chinese also believed that everything was made up of one of five elements: Wood, Fire, Earth, Metal and Water. Everyone is also ruled by one of these elements depending on his or her date of birth. You can look up your personal element in the Appendix (see page 113).

The five elements can be depicted in the form of cycles. The first of.these is called the Cycle of Production (see Figure 1G). Each element helps produce the next element in the cycle. Consequently, Wood burns and produces Fire. As Fire burns, it produces Earth. From the Earth we obtain Metal. Metal liquefies, which symbolically gives us Water. Water nurtures and produces Wood. Wood burns and creates Fire again. As you can see, this is a cycle that continually goes around and around.

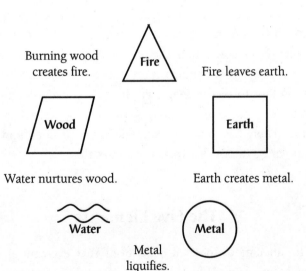

**Figure 1G: The Cycle of Production
of the Five Elements**

Ideally, you should have objects in your home that relate to both your personal element, and also the one that immediately precedes your element in the productive cycle. This is because the preceding element helps create your personal element. Water creates wood, for example.

The Destructive Cycle does the opposite. Fire can melt Metal. Metal can chop Wood. Wood drains from the Earth. Earth is able to dam, block and absorb water. Water can put out Fire.

These cycles are extremely useful in determining compatibility, and in helping to resolve relationship problems.

Fire

Color: Red

Shape: Triangular

Objects: Candles; anything red in color

Fire can warm, heat, and cheer. However, it can also burn and destroy. These two sides are also apparent in the makeup of people ruled by the fire element.

They make natural leaders, as they are warm and passionate, and they have the ability to motivate and inspire others. They love new ideas and concepts, and are constantly in search of change and variety. They experience many ups and downs in their lives as they seldom think ahead. Fire people are honest and expect everyone else to be the same. This naiveté can lead them into difficult situations. They are better at starting things than they are at finishing them. They are positive and optimistic. No matter what happens to them, they bounce back up again. They are loving, enthusiastic, and forever young at heart.

Earth

Color: Yellow

Shape: Square

Objects: Pottery, ceramics, crystals

Earth is nurturing and regenerative.

Earth people are stable, solid and reliable. They are patient, caring, and strong. They are practical, down-to-earth, and possess a warm sense of humor. They are logical and think before acting. They are also stubborn and resistant to change. They are able to instigate a project and carry it through to its conclusion. They are not as versatile as people born under the other elements. They prefer to do one task at a time, and do it properly. They do not necessarily need to be praised by others, as they receive enormous pleasure out of achieving a goal they have set for themselves. The pleasure of accomplishment is sufficient reward for them. They are prepared to work hard and long, and are frequently extremely successful financially.

Metal

Color: White

Shape: Round

Objects: Anything metallic

Metal is usually associated with gold, or money. However, it can also be related to a sword or dagger. Consequently, metal can be both productive and destructive.

Metal people are rigid, ambitious and single-minded. They believe in themselves and take themselves seriously. They seldom confide in others, preferring to solve their problems on their own. They are naturally independent and dislike being told what to do. They usually do well financially, as they possess an intriguing mixture of logic and intuition which helps them make good financial decisions. They take themselves seriously, and hate the thought of other people laughing at them.

Water

Color: Blue and black

Shape: Undulating, horizontal

Objects: Anything containing water

Water is closely related to creativity and the emotions. Water may be still and quiet in a pond, but in the ocean it can be fiercely destructive. Gentle rain nurtures the earth, but tor-rential hurricanes leave massive destruction in their wake.

Water people are often musical. Even if they do not sing or play an instrument, they are likely to have a good ear and enjoy listening to music. They are gentle people who do not like to hurt other people's feelings. All the same they are able to get their point of view across in quiet, subtle ways. They are naturally intuitive and are instantly aware of subtle nuances that people of other elements miss. They are flexible, adaptable, and easily influenced by others. They are emotional, sensitive and highly imaginative. They are usually creative but, being multi-talented, frequently find it hard to focus their efforts on just one creative field.

Wood

Color: Green

Shape: Rectangular

Objects: Living plants, flowers

Wood energy is expansive and all-encompassing. The ancient druids worshipped trees, as their roots went down to the underworld, their trunks lived in this world, and their branches reached up to the heavens.[6] Wood energy can be flexible as in a willow, or unyielding as in an oak.

Wood people are sociable and ambitious. They are good with details, and possess executive and managerial skills.

They enjoy planning ahead and usually have several long-range goals that they invariably achieve. They are highly moral and ethical, and despise people who do not have similar high standards. Wood people make good friends and employers as they are generous and kind-hearted. However, they often find it hard to express themselves as clearly as they would like and this can lead to frustration, anger, and impatience.

Schools of Feng Shui

For the first two and a half thousand years of its existence, there was just the one school of feng shui. This school used the geography of the landscape to make assessments. The ancient Chinese found that they lived better, more harmonious lives when their homes faced south, with hills behind them to protect them from the cold north winds. This is an example of using the formations of the landscape to decide on a suitable place to build. Not surprisingly, this is known as the Form School.

The first mention of the compass dates from about 206 B.C.E.[7] This invention allowed the Chinese to use the compass directions and to relate these to people's dates of birth. For the first time, feng shui was used for the specific needs of individuals. This is known as the Compass School.

The two systems developed independently, but for the last hundred years, most feng shui practitioners have used a combination of both schools.

There are a number of other schools of feng shui, but these are subgroupings of either the Form or Compass Schools. The Flying Star School, for instance, looks at future trends and is part of the Compass School.

Feng Shui spread around the world and was altered at different times to suit the needs of the people using it. For instance, in India, feng shui is known as Vastu Shastra, and uses Hindu, rather than Chinese, astrology.

In the following chapters we will examine all of these things in greater detail.

2

The Amazing Pa-kua

The pa-kua is derived from the magic square that Wu found in the markings on the tortoise shell some five thousand years ago. Each of the nine areas that make up the three-by-three magic square relate to a different aspect of our lives.

The first square, in the top left-hand corner, relates to Wealth. We activate this area to increase our income and become better off financially.

Next to the Wealth square is the Fame area. This relates to our reputation and standing in the community. However, it can also be activated in a variety of ways if we want to become famous.

The Marriage area is of prime concern to us in this book. It is in the top right-hand corner. We can activate this area to attract a relationship or to improve an existing relationship.

The Family and Health area is directly beneath the Wealth area on the left side of the pa-kua. We can activate this area when we are having family problems or when a member of the family is experiencing ill-health.

The center of the pa-kua is known as the Good Luck or Spiritual Center. Ch'i that is attracted here will spread

Wealth	Fame	Marriage
Family & Health	Good Luck Center	Children
Knowledge	Career	Mentors & Travel

The main entrance is always on this side of the square

Figure 2A: The Aspirations of the Pa-kua

throughout the rest of the house. This area is perfect for members of the household to do things together. It would make a good position for the dining room, for instance.

On the right-hand-side of the Good Luck Center is the Children area. We can activate this area if we are wanting children, or if we are having problems with children.

On the left-hand-side of the bottom row is the Knowledge area. This is a good place to store books and to study. We can activate this area when we are learning.

In the central position on the bottom row is the Career area. We can activate this part of the house to help us progress in our career and business life.

Finally, on the bottom right, is the Mentors and Travel area. Mentors are generally older people who can help us by offering advice and teaching us. We can attract these people to us by activating this area. We can also activate this part of the house when we want to travel (see Figure 2A).

The pa-kua is placed over a plan of our home, with the bottom edge of the magic square corresponding to the side of the house that the front door, or main entrance, is on. Consequently, if you come in the front door and go diagonally to the left as far as it is possible to go, you will find yourself in the Wealth area of your home. Head diagonally to the right and you will find yourself in the Marriage area, the most important area of the house for our purposes.

We can activate any area of the home we wish. This is usually done by increasing the amount of light in that part of the house, to attract additional ch'i into that area. We can also use a variety of feng shui remedies to achieve the results we are looking for. For instance, if we want more money, we might activate the Wealth area by including something in that part of the house that relates to our personal element. We might also have something metallic there, as metal relates to money. We might even keep an aquarium in this part of the house, as water means money, and fish represent forward progress. However, we need to do these things with care. For instance, if your personal element was Fire, you would not want an aquarium in the wealth area, as Water puts out Fire in the destructive cycle of the elements.

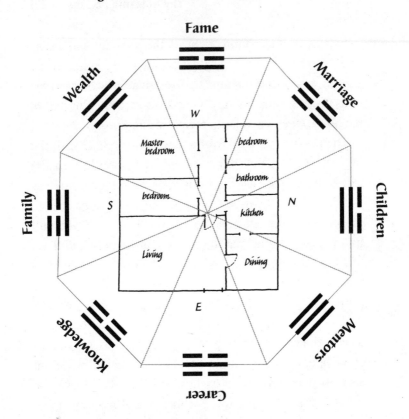

Figure 2B

The pa-kua fits neatly over homes that are square in shape (Figure 2B). The pa-kua also fits over rectangular-shaped houses (Figure 2C). However, we have problems with homes that are not regular in shape. For instance, the house shown in Figure 2C is missing the Marriage area. Needless to say, this will have an enormous effect on the marriage and relationship prospects of the people living in this house.

Fortunately, there are a number of remedies that can be used to rectify this problem. In Taiwan, the remedy would be to place a lamp on a pole in the garden in the position where the corner of the house would have been if the house had been regular in shape. In the West, people frequently hang wind chimes or plant trees in this position. However, it is not always possible to do this. If your home is an apartment, for instance, this position might be in the middle of your neighbor's living room!

Another remedy is to hang crystals in the windows of the two walls that mark off the missing section. This has the effect of symbolically squaring off the house.

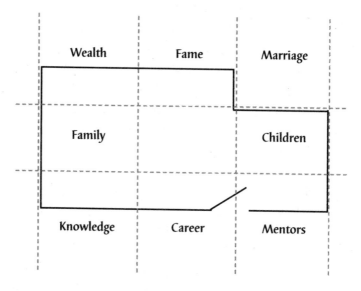

Figure 2C

If there are no windows on these walls, mirrors can be used. Mirrors are one of the most effective of feng shui remedies and, in this instance, a large mirror should be placed on each wall. The mirrors reflect back what they capture and, in effect, make the missing corner disappear. Mirrors should be as large as possible. Small mirrors symbolically cut off people's heads and feet, so, generally speaking, a large mirror is more effective from a feng shui point of view than a small one. However, sometimes the layout or decor of the room does not allow a large mirror to be used. In this case, there is no alternative, and a small mirror will have to be used.

A friend of mine rectified the missing marriage area in her apartment with two small mirrors, neither of which can be seen, as they are hidden by the back of her lounge suite. Within a month of putting them in place, she had her first date in more than a year. "I know they're there," she told me. And that is what makes the difference.

The pa-kua can be placed over the entire home, and it can also be used over each individual room inside the house. Consequently, another remedy for a missing marriage area in the home, is to activate that particular area in the individual rooms, particularly the bedroom.

Of course, you are likely to find that some rooms will be irregular in shape, and remedies will have to be used to rectify these. A man I know is in his mid-forties and still lives at home with his mother. He has never had a serious relationship. When I visited his home, I found that the bedroom he had slept in for his entire life was missing the marriage area. I suggested that he place crystals in the two windows to remedy this lack, but within a few days his mother had taken them down. She knows nothing about feng shui, but must have intuitively realized that she was in danger of losing her precious son if the crystals remained in position. Until he does something to rectify this missing part of his room, I am sure he will remain single.

How to Activate the Marriage Sector

The most important marriage sector of your home is the one indicated by the pa-kua placed over the entire house. Next in importance is the Marriage sector in your bedroom, followed by the living room and then the other rooms in your home.

Start by increasing the light in this part of your home. If the marriage sector of your home is gloomy and badly lit, any relationships are likely to be sluggish and apathetic. You may be able to increase the amount of light by opening blinds and curtains during the day. At night, keep this part of the house well lit, until you are ready for bed. Crystals are an effective way of attracting light into any area that you wish to activate.

Remove any clutter from this area. Clutter can take a variety of forms. A pile of old magazines that are gathering dust is a good example. If the magazines were being used and referred to on a regular basis, they would not be considered clutter provided they were stored neatly.

A lady I knew kept several cardboard boxes containing the financial records of a business she used to own in the

Marriage sector of her bedroom. You can imagine how lacking in excitement her love life was!

Another lady I know complained that her love life was boring. It turned out that her husband would undress for bed in the Marriage sector of their bedroom and leave his clothes all over the floor. This created clutter for several hours every night in a vital part of the room. She and her husband could not believe the change in their relationship once he started putting his clothes away, rather than leaving them on the floor.

Place something in this part of the house that relates to your personal element, or the one that precedes your element in the productive cycle of elements. For instance, if your element is Wood, you might place an attractive-looking potted plant in this area. Alternatively, you might have a small aquarium (as Water precedes Wood in the productive cycle. This means that Water nurtures and nourishes Wood). You have to ensure that whatever it is you place in this area is looked after. A potted plant has to be watered regularly. If you belong to the Metal element you might choose to have a silver figurine, or some other metallic ornament in this position. Again, you would have to ensure that it was kept dusted and clean. A dusty ornament in the Marriage sector indicates a tired, lackluster relationship. Keep everything clean, fresh, and sparkling and you will bring those qualities into your relationships.

If you are already in a relationship, keep something in this area that relates to both of your elements. The one exception to this occurs if you are living with someone who has an element that is next to yours on the destructive cycle. (The destructive cycle is: Fire destroys Metal, Metal cuts Wood, Wood drains from the Earth, Earth dams and blocks Water, and Water puts out Fire.) In this instance, you need to have something that relates to the element that comes between them in the productive cycle.

For instance, if you belong to the Fire element and your partner belongs to Metal, you should have something that relates to the Earth element in the Marriage sector of your bedroom. (This is because Earth comes between Fire and Metal in the productive cycle.)

Another example would be if you belonged to the Water element and your partner belonged to Earth. In this instance, a metallic object in the Marriage sector would neutralize the destructive aspects of the two elements, and help create a smoother, more harmonious relationship.

Finally, you can attract a relationship by displaying anything that you feel represents love and romance. This varies enormously from person to person. You might choose to hang up a poster showing a couple walking hand in hand across a deserted beach. You might have a jewelry box that is shaped like a heart.

One lady I know has a bowl of fresh fruit in the marriage sector of her home. When she was a small child, she was in love with a boy who lived nearby. He frequently presented her with an apple or orange, and even today, thirty years later, fresh fruit symbolizes love to her.

The Marriage sector should appear attractive and welcoming. Consequently, it is a good idea to keep items of furniture and other objects in this location that you consider attractive. If this part of the house is appealing and welcoming, you will want to spend time here. By doing this, you will subconsciously send positive energies out into the universe which will attract the right person to you.

In many cases, activating the Marriage sector brings instantaneous, almost miraculous, results. However, it does not work like this for everyone. Be patient. Remain confident that because you have activated, and look after, this part of your home that you are attracting the right person into your life.

Spend time in the Marriage sector of your home. Think only pleasant thoughts when you are there. Do not spend time in the Marriage sector when you are feeling unhappy, stressed or angry. You want this part of your home to be an oasis of peace and tranquillity. We attract to us what we think about. Consequently, this is a good area to sit in and think about the love and happiness that is coming to you.

3

How to Attract Love to Your Home

We all want love in our lives. Some people find it easily, but for others it appears endlessly elusive. Fortunately, there are many things that we can do to our home environments that will attract peace, harmony—and love.

Front Door

Your main entrance is, in effect, the mouth to your home. Most of the ch'i comes in through the main entrance. The door should be neither too large nor too small for the size of the house. If it is too large, the occupants will feel small. If it is too small for the size of the house, the ch'i will be constricted and find it hard to come in.

The front door should also be easy to find. If your visitors find it hard to determine your main entrance, the ch'i will also. Consequently, it should appear welcoming, and people standing at the entrance should be able to see a glimpse of part of the interior (see Figure 3A, next page).

Figure 3A: A welcoming front entrance

Make sure that the front door is protected from shars, or poison arrows. The worst shar possible occurs when a street heads in a straight line directly towards your main entrance. Fortunately, as you know, a shar ceases to exist if you cannot see it. Consequently, a hedge, fence or group of trees can be used to symbolically make the shar disappear. If this is not possible, a pa-kua mirror can be used to reflect the shar back where it came from.

A path leading in a straight line from the sidewalk to the front door also creates a shar that affects the whole house. Shars like this can be easily remedied as they are on your own property. If you can, replace the path with one that gently curves. Alternatively, you could create a path that heads in a straight line towards the house beside the front door, and then turns at a ninety degree angle towards the entrance (Figure 3B).

In ancient China they believed that ghosts could travel only in straight lines. If your front path curves or has sharp bends in it, ghosts will not be able to come into your home through the front door.

You can make the path more attractive and welcoming with gardens of flowers and small plants. This both creates and encourages the ch'i, which is attracted to anything beautiful in nature.

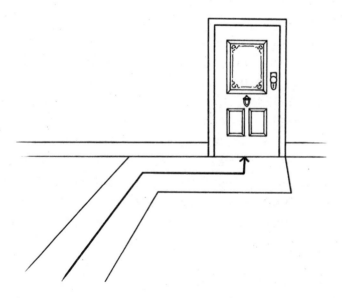

Figure 3B: Front door shar remedy

Animals are frequently used in feng shui for protection. If you feel the need for some form of security, you may want to place a pair of stone animals outside your front door. Lions are commonly used for this purpose.

It is considered bad feng shui for visitors to arrive at the front door and immediately face a staircase heading upwards. This is because it confuses the ch'i, which does not know whether to stay on the ground level or head upstairs. It is also believed that with an entrance like this, occupants will head directly upstairs to their private rooms, rather than socialize with the other occupants.

A chandelier or hanging crystal acts as a remedy for this. The chandelier should be hung from the ceiling approximately halfway between the entrance and the foot of the stairs.

It is also bad feng shui for your visitors to see the back door from the front door. This means the ch'i comes in through the front door and immediately leaves again through the back door. You can rectify this by using a screen to conceal the back door.

Sometimes, the back door is visible at the end of a long hallway, which creates an internal shar. Ch'i speeds up when it travels in straight lines. We can slow it down in one of two ways. We can hang up three or more mirrors, alternating them on opposite sides of the hallway. This forces the ch'i to flow in a wave-like manner, which slows it down. Alternatively, we can hang crystals from the ceiling, which has the same effect of attracting the ch'i and slowing it down.

It is bad feng shui to see a toilet or bathroom from the front door. This is because water means money in feng shui. Consequently, it is bad feng shui to see water dripping or flushing away as, in effect, we are watching money disappear. Toilets and bathrooms create negative ch'i and should be situated in out-of-the-way parts of the house where they become almost invisible. If these rooms are visible from the front door, make sure that you keep the doors shut at all times. You might want to place a mirror on these doors as well, to symbolically make the room disappear.

Living Room

Your living room should be reasonably close to the front door. It should be warm and welcoming. There should also be items on display that reflect the interests of members of the household.

There are power positions in every room. These are chairs and couches placed in a position where whoever sits in them can see the main entrance to the room without turning his or her head. In the East, it is considered polite to offer these seats to your visitors and to take a less auspicious seat for yourself.

If you live alone, you should ensure that you use all of the different seats in the living room and dining room. If you habitually use just one chair, you are subconsciously sending out messages that you do not want the other seats to be occupied. Consequently, if you want to attract love into your life, you should vary your seating position as often as possible.

One woman I know suffered desperately from loneliness until I encouraged her to use the other chairs in her home. She now has a new relationship, and has also joined a group that plays bridge in each others' homes. She is now so busy and happy that she has no time to feel lonely.

Naturally, special attention should be paid to the Marriage sector of this room. Display attractive ornaments and anything that reminds you of love and romance in this area. If you are in a relationship that lacks passion, try placing something in this area that is red in color. This will help revitalize the relationship.

Kitchen

The most important part of the kitchen is the oven. This used to be considered the seat of the family's wealth. It is important that anyone working at the oven can see anyone entering the room without turning his or her head. It is believed that people coming into the room behind the cook's back can surprise the cook, and consequently affect the quality of the food. Mirrors can act as a remedy if the cook's back faces the main entrance to the room.

The refrigerator should be kept well-stocked. This signifies wealth and abundance. An almost empty refrigerator indicates a lack of abundance, and this refers to your love life as well as every other aspect of your life.

Make sure that there are no leaky taps in the kitchen. They indicate money flowing away from you. Pipes that carry water should not be visible for the same reason.

Dining Room

The dining room should appear spacious. The most important item of furniture in this room is the dining room table. People sitting at the table should be able to get in and out without feeling restricted in any way. If you live on your own, make sure that you sit at every position around the table to encourage visitors.

This room is related to abundance. You may want to hang a large mirror in this room. This is to reflect the meals on the table, making them appear to double in number.

A bowl of fresh fruit on the table relates to love, as well as plentifulness and abundance. Make sure that you eat the fruit and replace the supply regularly.

Bathroom and Toilet

These should be in an inconspicuous part of the house. This provides privacy for the people using them. Ideally, they should be on an outside wall, as they create negative ch'i. A toilet in the middle of the house spreads negative ch'i throughout the home.

It is better feng shui for the bathroom and toilet to be separate rooms. If they are combined, ensure that a half-wall or partition divides the two, to allow a degree of privacy.

En suite bathrooms are very popular in the West, but are considered bad in feng shui terms. The negative ch'i created spreads into the bedroom. Also, they frequently have the effect of turning a square or oblong bedroom into an irregular shape, which causes feng shui problems.

The bathroom and toilet should never be placed in the Wealth sector of the house. Naturally, water drains away from these rooms, and as water represents money in feng shui, these rooms in the Wealth sector indicate a gradual diminishing of wealth.

Ideally, these rooms should also not be in the Marriage sector as they then represent love and romance symbolically flushing down the toilet.

Fortunately, there is a remedy if your bathroom is located in either the Wealth or Marriage sectors. First, the doors should be kept closed as much as possible. Place mirrors on two opposing walls inside the bathroom, as this symbolically causes the room to disappear. Some authorities suggest that four mirrors should be used, and I would recommend this in situations where it is practical. Finally, a mirror should be hung on the outside of the door, which has the symbolic effect of making the room appear invisible from the outside.

Bedroom

This is the most important room in the house from a relationship point of view, which is why I have left it until last.

We want to encourage as much ch'i as possible into this room during the day, as we all spend several hours asleep here at night. Consequently, blinds should be opened during the daytime to allow light in. Windows should be opened, if possible. Sunlight is good, but we do not want direct sunlight on the bed itself. This is because it is believed to overactivate the bed and make it hard to get to sleep. However, if you are progressing with a new relationship, an overactivated bed might be exactly what you want!

The bed should touch a wall to gain support. The foot of the bed should not point directly towards the main entrance to the room (Figure 3C). This is known as the coffin position. In ancient China, people were buried accord-

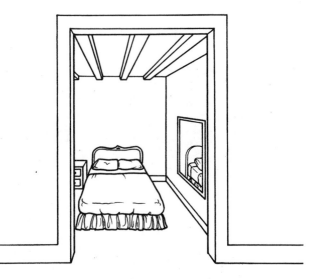

Figure 3C: Bed in coffin position

ing to their horoscope, and sometimes had to wait as long as a month before they could be buried. Their coffins were lined up in the courtyards of the temples. When Chinese people see the foot of a bed pointing directly towards the door it reminds them of this coffin position.

The bed should be placed in a position where the occupants can see anyone coming in the main entrance to the room without turning their heads more than ninety degrees (Figure 3D). We are at our most vulnerable while asleep, and this traditional feng shui concept reflects that fear. Of course, a mirror can be used when there is no other convenient place to put the bed.

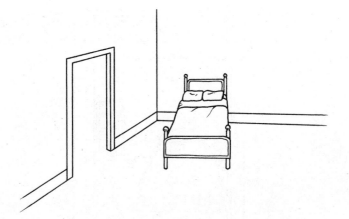

Figure 3D: Position of bed to entrance

Figure 3E: Beams above bed

Overhead beams act as shars and are considered to be negative in every room of the house. They are particularly bad in the bedroom, as it is believed that the people sleeping below them will ultimately suffer ill health in the parts of their bodies that are crossed by the beams (Figure 3E).

If there is no alternative, it is better for the beams to go lengthwise down the bed, rather than across it. However, beams that go lengthwise can adversely affect relationships by providing a symbolic barrier between the two people.

The best remedy is get rid of the beams, either by removing them completely, or by lowering the ceiling to make them disappear. Alternatively, two bamboo flutes can be hung by red thread or ribbon from every beam to create a traditional feng shui remedy.

You cannot have too many mirrors in your home from a feng shui point of view. However, they need to be placed with care in the bedroom. In fact, some feng shui practitioners say that mirrors should not be used in the bedroom at all. This is because the reflections they make give the illusion of extra people in the room, and this can prove disruptive to a close relationship. The worst position for a mirror to face is the foot of the bed. There are two reasons for this. It is believed to have an adverse affect on close relationships. In traditional feng shui it is also believed that if you wake up in the middle of the night and sit up in bed you might see your reflection in the mirror and think that it is a ghost.

My wife and I have just one mirror in our bedroom, and it is placed so that it cannot reflect the bed. If you have concerns about hanging mirrors in your bedroom, you may find it better to place them in the bathroom or dressing room, where they can do no harm.

Pastel colors and soft lights can help create a restful, relaxed atmosphere in this room. Harsh, strong lights in the bedroom are believed to create stress and tension.

4

Feng Shui Compatibility

Compatibility is a fascinating subject. Why are we drawn to some people, and repelled by others? Why do some people choose a succession of highly unsuitable partners, while other people find the perfect partner while still in high school? The subject is a fascinating mystery.

Feng shui can help bring people into your life, but it is up to you to determine which one of them is likely to be the best person for you.

One method of determining compatibility is through the five elements. We are naturally more drawn to people who belong to the elements on either side of ours on the productive cycle than we are to people belonging to the other elements. We are also likely to have relationship problems with people who belong to the elements on either side of ours on the destructive cycle.

Here is a listing of the type of relationship each combination is likely to have (Refer to the Appendix on page 113 to determine your—and your partner's—element):

Fire/Fire

Fire people are enthusiastic, positive and optimistic. When two Fire people get together it can be an extremely strong combination. Fire people can bring out the best in other Fire people, frequently making this an enduring combination where neither partner ever gets bored with the other.

Fire/Earth

This is a harmonious combination, as both partners are good at stimulating and exciting the other. The excellent imagination of Fire, coupled with the sensuality of Earth, create a relationship that can succeed on every level.

Fire/Metal

Fire has the power to melt metal, making this a difficult combination. The Metal person will try to impose his or her will on the Fire person with disastrous results. The Fire person's ego will gradually wear down the Metal person. Both are competitive and will try to outdo the other. Fortunately, both people have a good sense of humor which can be used to defuse difficult situations. These people need to have something from the Earth element in their home to neutralize some of the negative effects of this combination.

Fire/Water

The Fire and Water combination is a difficult one, as water puts out fire. However, water can add creativity to the enthusiasm and energy of fire, and fire people have the power to inspire people of the water element. Although both partners have good communication skills, they will find it hard to get their deepest feelings across to the other person. This couple will need something from the Wood element in their home to neutralize the negative aspects of this combination.

Fire/Wood

Fire and Wood is a harmonious combination. The Wood person gives stability to the impulsiveness of the Fire. The Fire person's energy and enthusiasm can motivate the Wood person to greater success than would be possible on his or her own. Both are optimistic, outward-looking people who enjoy exploring new ideas and concepts.

Earth/Earth

This is a highly positive combination, as both partners will be concerned about maintaining a high standard of living and attending to the needs of the other. This relationship may seem dull to outsiders, but in reality it will be deep, strong, and passionate. Problems could arise as both can be stubborn. However, there is love and goodwill on both sides and these temporary hiccups will invariably be resolved.

Earth/Metal

This is an excellent combination, as both partners will support, respect and admire the other. The Metal person is naturally patient, something that is essential in this relationship as Earth always takes time to make up his or her mind. The Metal person will expose his or her Earth partner to wider, more exciting opportunities. The Earth person will nurture the Metal's financial ambitions, ensuring that the relationship becomes financially secure, as well.

Earth/Water

This can be a difficult combination, as each partner is likely to hurt the other one emotionally. Earth provides the stability that water lacks, but the stubbornness of Earth will be a constant turnoff for the more sensitive Water person. (Incidentally, this can be an extremely powerful business combination, as the creativity of Water, coupled with the commonsense, materialistic approach of Earth invariably does well.) This couple will need to keep something from the Metal element in their home to help neutralize any potential difficulties.

Earth/Wood

Wood drains from the Earth, making this a difficult combination. Earth is stable, conservative and cautious, while Wood is progressive, communicative and expansive. Once they resolve to help each other, rather than bicker and squabble, this combination can be successful, as long as they are prepared to express their feelings openly. This couple should have something from the Fire element in their home to help neutralize the negative aspects of this combination.

Metal/Metal

This combination works well as both partners innately understand the other. They will experience the usual ups and downs of all relationships, but are prepared to work together for the common good whenever necessary. To an outsider, this relationship may not appear to be a close one. This is because Metal people usually prefer to go their own way and do their own thing. However, they work exceptionally well with other people from the same element, and create a strong, long-lasting relationship.

Metal/Water

This is a powerful relationship in which both partners are significantly helped by the other. Both partners are guided by their intuition and feelings and will be able to communicate effectively with each other at a subliminal level. The Metal person teaches his or her Water partner not to be so easily influenced by others. The Water person helps the Metal partner to express his or her feelings more effectively and to go with the flow, rather than stubbornly hang on to the old.

Metal/Wood

This is a potentially difficult relationship, as both partners will want to dominate, and each will be adamant that his or her way is how certain tasks should be done. Wood will want company, but Metal will be perfectly happy on his or her own, and these times of solitude will prove frustrating to the naturally gregarious, outgoing Wood. Both people will be highly responsible. Wood is easy to get along with and will probably adapt to Metal's need for time on his or her own. Metal frequently will be frustrated by Wood's need for perfection. If Metal bends a little and goes along with Wood's ideas, the relationship will work, but there will need to be a great deal of give and take on both sides.

Water/Water

The Water-Water relationship can often appear to be made in heaven. Both partners will have a strong, deep intuitive affinity for the other, and will instinctively understand the other's needs and desires. This combination strengthens both partners' resolve and makes them less easily influenced by others. Each person gains confidence and self-esteem from the other.

Water/Wood

This is a highly positive combination as Water nurtures Wood and helps it grow and flourish. Wood helps Water by giving it stability and a sense of purpose. Water gives Wood a sense of compassion, and also encourages the other to express him or herself better. Wood boosts up the Water, who can be prone to moodiness. Both partners are honest, ethical, and empathetic. They have an intuitive bond that will continue to develop and grow.

Wood/Wood

This is a highly active, compatible combination. Wood people are naturally busy, active people who like to be involved in everything. This is compounded when two Wood people get together, and they are likely to be involved in many mutual interests, as well as their careers and a multitude of individual interests. This combination can be exhausting for others to witness, but the two Wood people thrive on it. Both are basically secure individuals, who trust the other implicitly. They are patient, trusting, tolerant people who are ready to help the other at any time.

Naturally, these compatibility assessments do not give the complete picture. You need to have complete charts drawn up to do that. Chinese astrology is a complex art, and what we have done here is similar to determining compatibility using the sun signs of Western astrology.

However, I have found the relationships between the elements extremely useful in practice. They can help you decide whether or not you wish to proceed with a new relationship, and enable you to understand your partner better in an existing relationship.

5

Further into the Pa-kua

In Chapter Two we used the pa-kua to determine the nine positions in each home. This is known as the Aspirations of the Pa-kua, and is the most commonly used method of feng shui evaluation in Hong Kong.

Now we can take the pa-kua several steps further. Each of the nine boxes that make up the three-by-three magic square also relate to a specific direction, a color, and a trigram from the I Ching. The I Ching, also known as *The Book of Changes,* is the oldest book of China and has had a major influence on Chinese thought, philosophy, and culture for thousands of years. The whole purpose of the I Ching was to help people understand and become attuned to the endless cycles and rhythms of the universe.

The Eight Trigrams

The I Ching uses a binary system of eight trigrams (see Figure 5A, next page). These are diagrams or figures made up of three broken or unbroken lines. A broken line is described as

51

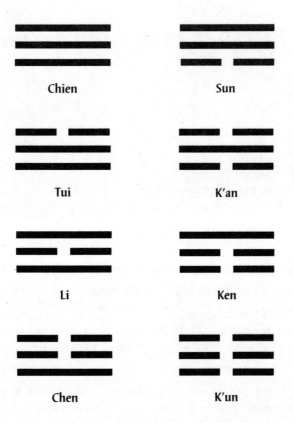

Figure 5A: The Eight Trigrams

being yin, or feminine, while an unbroken line is termed yang, or masculine. Each trigram has a meaning and a position inside the pa-kua (Figure 5B).

There are two different combinations of the trigrams, known as the Former Heaven Sequence and the Latter Heaven Sequence. The first of these was devised by Wu of Hsia (the first emperor of China, who found the tortoise that contained the magic square on its shell). This arrangement depicted a rather idealistic view of the universe. The Latter Heaven Sequence was devised by the Duke of Wen in about 1143 B.C.E. This is a more practical arrangement of the trigrams, and is the one that is generally used today.

	South	
SE		SW
Sun 4 **Wind**	**Li** 9 **Fire**	**K'un** 2 **Earth**
Chen 3 **Thunder**	**Spiritual** 5 **Center**	**Tui** 7 **Lake**
Ken 8 **Mountain**	**K'an** 1 **Water**	**Chien** 6 **Heaven**
NE	North	NW

Figure 5B: Pa-kua

The trigrams are placed in the positions on the magic square shown in Figure 5B. The pa-kua that we placed over our house in Chapter Two did not use compass directions. By using a compass, we can learn a great deal more about ourselves and our homes. More importantly, we can use that information to improve our love lives.

The Chinese invented the compass.[1] They considered south to be the most auspicious direction. This is not surprising, as the cold harsh winds come from the North. Consequently, South is placed at the top position of their compass. Consequently, in Figure 5B, Li, in the top position, is actually in the South, and K'an is in the North.

You will need a compass to correctly align this new magic square over a plan of your home. The magic square will be placed in exactly the same position as it was in Chapter Two (Figure 2A), only if your front door faces North. This is because we aligned the front door with the bottom row of the magic square to create what is known as the Aspirations of the Pa-kua.

Chien

CHIEN - the Creative

Direction:	North-West
Symbol:	Heaven
Keyword:	Strength and Prosperity
Element:	Metal
Color:	Purple
Yin/Yang:	Yang

Chien is comprised of three (yang) unbroken lines. It relates to the head of the household, usually the father, and the rooms that he would be likely to use, such as the study, office, or main bedroom. It also relates to Heaven, the sky, and the stars. It is strong and is associated with energy, ambition, and endurance. It is also associated with originality, power, coldness, and prosperity.

K'un

K'UN - the Receptive

Direction: South-West

Symbol: the Earth

Keyword: Preparation and Obedience

Element: Earth

Color: Black

Yin/Yang: Yin

K'un is made up of three broken (yin) lines. This naturally relates to maternal qualities, and symbolizes the mother and the rooms she would be most likely to use, such as the kitchen and sewing room. It also relates to devotion, receptivity, protectiveness, faithfulness, and obedience. It symbolizes close relationships, particularly that of husband and wife.

Chen

CHEN - the Arousing

Direction:	East
Symbol:	Thunder
Keyword:	Beginnings and Progress
Element:	Wood
Color:	Orange
Yin/Yang:	Yang

Chen is made up of two broken (yin) lines above an unbroken (yang) line. It represents the eldest son. Consequently, a good place for his bedroom is in the East. It relates to decisiveness, unexpected occurrences, impulsiveness, and experimentation. It is also associated with speed and movement.

Sun

SUN - the Gentle

Direction:	South-East
Symbol:	Wind
Keyword:	Development
Element:	Wood
Color:	White
Yin/Yang:	Yin

Sun is made up of two unbroken (yang) lines above a broken (yin) line. It represents the eldest daughter. Consequently, her bedroom should be in the South-east part of the house. It relates to a good mind and inner strength. It is also associated with flexibility and the ability to fit into any type of situation.

K'an

K'AN - the Abysmal

Direction: North

Symbol: Water

Keyword: Entrapment

Element: Water

Color: Red

Yin/Yang: Yang

K'an comprises an unbroken (yang) line between two broken (yin) lines. It represents the middle son. It relates to hard work, drive, and ambition. However, it is also associated with guile, secrets, and danger. North is considered a negative direction in traditional feng shui, as cold winds and imaginary demons come from the North.

Li

LI - the Clinging

Direction:	South
Symbol:	Fire
Keyword:	Fame
Element:	Fire
Color:	Yellow
Yin/Yang:	Yin

Li comprises a broken (yin) line between two unbroken (yang) lines. It represents the middle daughter. It relates to beauty, laughter, warmth, and success. Obviously, this is a good location for her bedroom. It also relates to communication, enlightenment, and clarity of thought. This area is a good location for the living room where happiness and laughter would abound. The South is traditionally considered the most positive direction in feng shui.

Ken

KEN - Keeping Still

Direction:	North-East
Symbol:	Mountain
Keyword:	Pause
Element:	Earth
Color:	Green
Yin/Yang:	Yang

Ken is made up of two broken (yin) lines beneath an unbroken (yang) line. It represents the youngest son. Ken relates to solidity, stability, and success through study and learning. It is also associated with modesty, carefulness, and peace and quiet.

Tui

TUI - the Joyful

Direction:	West
Symbol:	Lake
Keyword:	Joy
Element:	Lake
Color:	Blue
Yin/Yang:	Yin

Tui is made up of a broken (yin) line above two unbroken (Yang) lines. It represents the youngest daughter. Tui relates to happiness, pleasure, sensuality, joy, and contentment. It is also associated with entertainment and recreation.

Each area of the house has a role to play in your love life and subsequent happiness.

SUN - Wind

Keyword: Trust

The symbol for Sun is Wind. In fact, many people refer to the eight trigrams by their symbol names, rather than their traditional Chinese trigram names. This is because the symbol names create a mental picture that helps understanding. "Feng shui" means "wind and water." We need both of these to survive. Without air we cannot breathe. Air can be both moving and stagnant. When this part of your house is stagnant, your relationship will also feel stifled and dead. Neither do we want the relationship to be like a torrential wind. Although this would be exciting and stimulating for a short while, it would soon become too exhausting and would wear you out.

This part of your house relates to harmony, happiness, trust, and forward progress. You will need to activate this part of your home if you want to encourage more of these qualities in your relationship.

Wind chimes are a logical remedy here. When they make music, you will be aware that the wind is flowing freely through this part of your home. Incidentally, some feng shui practitioners say that wind chimes should never be used inside the house. This is a matter of personal preference. I have used wind chimes inside my own home for many years and have found them extremely beneficial. If you would rather not have them indoors, place them outside, close to the Sun area of your home.

You can also use any of the other remedies. Try placing something that relates to the personal elements of you and your partner in this area. If you do not have a relationship, use something that relates to the element that precedes yours on the productive cycle of elements. This will help create harmony, contentment—and ultimately love—in your personal element.

Occupants of your home are likely to suffer bad luck and frequent disappointments if the Sun area is missing.

LI - Fire

Keyword: Closeness, Clarity

Fire provides warmth, inspiration and enthusiasm. Naturally, too much fire can leave havoc in its wake, and too little fire marks the end of many relationships.

Activating this part of your home can help you and your partner rekindle your passion and love for each other, and open up new paths of communication. When you come across two lovers who exist only for each other, you see a couple with exactly the right amount of fire in their lives.

This is the part of the house to activate if every area of your relationship is going well, except for your sex life. If your sex life is humdrum or almost non-existent, place attractive red lights and ornaments in the Li part of your home. Do not expect your sex life to be transformed right away. However, you will notice a gradual improvement. Usually, you will start to notice that the two of you are communicating better, and at a deeper level than before.

This is a good start, and before long, you will find your sex life improving more and more.

Red objects are useful in this area, even if you have no partner. They will stimulate you and make you more attractive to others.

White lights, candles and clear quartz crystals help you become more in tune with the other people in your life. They can also open the doors for greater communication and self-expression.

When the Li area of the home is missing the occupants tend to lack confidence and self-esteem. Their sex lives will be unsatisfactory and humdrum. They will also be overly concerned about what other people think of them.

K'UN - Earth

Keyword: Feelings

Earth makes us feel safe, secure, and nurtured. Consequently, this part of the house is closely related to feelings. Some people are overly emotional, while others seem cold and aloof, completely out of touch with their feelings.

Naturally, we want to be able to express our feelings openly and honestly. We also want our partner to do the same. If one person is always angry, possessive, jealous, sulky or uncommunicative the relationship is doomed, unless that person can learn to become more in tune with his or her emotions.

The remedy for all emotional difficulties is to activate this area of your home. Anything from the earth will suffice. Pottery, ceramics and crystals all work well in this area.

This is a good position to display photographs of you and your partner enjoying happy, loving times together.

Place red objects in this area if you find it hard to express your feelings. (Fire creates Earth in the Cycle of Production.)

This area also relates to intuition. Consequently, you are likely to find your psychic awareness developing once you activate this part of your home.

When the K'un area is missing in a home, the occupants will have little interest in maintaining the garden. Men will have difficulty in their relationships with women, and women will not enjoy living in the house.

CHEN - Thunder

Keyword: Outside influences

Thunder is a good name for this part of your home. Outside influences can wreak havoc in our lives, sometimes coming with the power and suddenness of a clap of thunder. Members of our own family can sometimes be among the worst of outside influences. If you have ever had a relationship with someone who members of your family disapproved of, you will be aware of the subtle, powerful, intrusive effects of thunder. Coworkers and friends may feel they are doing the right thing in trying to break up what they feel is a bad relationship, but the result is often confusion, distrust, stress, and worry.

The antidote is to activate this part of your home. Display anything here that feels warm, protective and nurturing. Objects that relate to your personal elements will also help. Peaceful, calm colors, such as blue and green can also be used to good effect. For instance, an aquamarine crystal can help absorb the disharmony and confusion, leaving you with feelings of peace and contentment.

Be gentle on the people who try to intrude in your love life. They are doing it because they care for you and your happiness. In this instance, they are not helping at all. They are simply adding to your stress and aggravation. Tell them gently that you know what you are doing, and if you want their advice, you will ask for it.

When the Chen area of the home is missing, the occupants will feel listless and lacking in energy.

SPIRITUAL CENTER

Keyword: The Inner You

The very center of the pa-kua does not have a trigram. This part of the home is known as the spiritual center, and is the perfect place for members of the household to spend time with each other. It is also an excellent place to become in tune with oneself. If you are searching for a relationship, or are having problems within a relationship, spend some quality time by yourself in this part of your home. This is a good place for meditation.

If you do not know how to meditate, simply relax here. Take several deep breaths, close your eyes, and consciously relax different parts of your body. When you feel totally relaxed, concentrate on your breathing and let your mind wander where it will. You may find answers to different questions mysteriously coming to you. You may find an inner peace that you never knew existed. At the very least, you will open your eyes refreshed, relaxed, and ready to carry on with your life.

Spending time on your own in the spiritual center of your home can be very beneficial to your physical, mental and spiritual self.

TUI - Lake

Keyword: Sensuality, sexuality, excitement

As a child I spent many vacations beside a beautiful lake. I loved it in all its moods, from still, calm, indigo tranquillity to raging torrent with azure waves pounding on the beach. Tui is very much like this. It reflects all the joys and delights of physical passion. However, it also reflects stale, stagnant relationships where all passion has died.

If you keep attracting the wrong people to you, this area of your home will need rectifying. Spend time in the spiritual center of your home and ask yourself what it is that you desire in the perfect partner. It might be helpful to write your answers down over a period of several days.

A friend of mine invariably chose total losers who would use her, frequently abuse her, and then leave. She claimed that these men were exciting because they were "different" and lived outside the bounds of the world she grew up in. However, when she sat down and worked out what sort of man she really wanted, the description that came was totally different. It took her a while to accept this, but once she started sending out the right energies, the right man came into her life.

If this is your problem, place flowers and potted plants in this part of your home. Hang crystals or wind chimes that reflect the color of the element that precedes yours in the Productive Cycle of Elements. Sit in this area every day and read the description you have written of your ideal partner. Keep your thoughts positive, and you will ultimately attract this person to you.

If your relationship used to be passionate, but all physical attraction has long since vanished, rectify this area. This area relates to sexual problems and difficulties as well. Red candles and crystals in this area can do wonders to increase sexual vitality and to re-ignite formerly passionate relationships. Red curtains and furniture also help, but make sure that it is not overdone. Too much red can create aggression, rather than passion, and can also cause partners to seek sexual satisfaction elsewhere.

If the Tui area of the home is missing the occupants will find it hard to save money. They will be inclined to spend it as soon as they receive it, saving nothing for the future.

KEN - Mountain

Keyword: Communication

Mountains are natural boundaries. We have to either climb over them or get around them to proceed. Communication is an essential part of any relationship. It is hard to imagine any relationship surviving without at least some degree of communication between the two parties. Without communication, it is as if each person is on an opposite side of a mountain. Sometimes we have to climb that mountain to reach and communicate with the person on the other side.

Communication is never easy, of course. You may talk and talk and talk, but if your partner is not listening, you are wasting your time. Communication is a two-way process.

Honesty is also essential. There is no point in communicating at all if no one is telling the truth.

Effective communication brings people closer together, and lack of communication forces people apart. If you are having communication problems in your relationship (and they could be of a physical, verbal or emotional nature) you will need to enhance this part of your home in some way.

Anything that is pink or yellow in color makes a suitable remedy. If one person in the relationship is having problems in communication, display something of the color that precedes his or her color on the Productive Cycle of Elements.

You may think that this is not likely to be a problem area if you are not in a relationship. In fact, it might well be the reason why you are on your own. If you think that communicating your innermost feelings may have been a problem in the past, or may be a problem in the future, hang up a yellow wind chime or display some yellow-colored flowers in this area.

When the Ken area of the home is missing, female occupants could suffer from gynecological problems and may have difficulty in conceiving.

K'AN - Water

Keyword: Love, Romance

We cannot live without water. Some people claim that we cannot live without love, either. Water can be both gentle and calm, and also a raging torrent. Water is fluid, always moving and finding new paths to take. K'an is also concerned with movement. Its aim is to propel relationships forward, to jump-start relationships that have become stuck in a rut, and to help forge new relationships.

If you have been in a relationship for a while, but your partner is afraid to commit, activate this part of your home and see what happens. If you have been on your own for too long, activate this area and prepare for a new relationship. If your relationship has become staid and boring, activate this area and allow love to blossom anew.

K'an and Tui both relate to Water. Tui is mainly concerned with physical passion. K'an is interested in love in all its various forms. This includes lovemaking, of course, but it also involves the more spiritual aspects of love.

Anything that is pink, rose, or red can be used to activate this part of your home. An acquaintance of mine was given a large piece of rose quartz. I suggested she place it in the K'an area of her home, and within a month she had two men courting her.

Other remedies include plants. Living plants are preferred, but artificial plants will work just as well, provided they are looked after and kept free of dust. Dusty plants in this area relate to dull, stale, boring partners. Dried flowers have had all the water drained out of them and should never be used in feng shui. As you know, "feng shui" means "wind and water."

Wind chimes and mobiles, preferably painted green, pink, or red, work well in this area. All crystals are good. Encourage the ch'i in with plenty of light and fresh air.

When the K'an area of the home is missing, the occupants will suffer from periods of ill-health.

CHIEN - Heaven

Keyword: Friendship

This area is one of the most important places in the home as the happiest people in the world are those with partners who are both lovers and friends. Most people need help in this area, and activating this area can improve almost all relationships. Naturally, this area is not restricted solely to making friends with your lover. It can also be activated to encourage more friends of both sexes into your life, and to improve your relationships with existing friends.

You should pay particular attention to this part of your home if you are always too busy to spend time with your friends. The same thing applies if you find it hard to make friends. You may have dozens of acquaintances, but no one who you can call a real friend.

Maybe, because of past experiences, you find it hard to trust others. This is common, particularly if you have been let down by others. Activating this area can help you reach out more easily in the future.

Perhaps you are in a relationship where you are doing all the giving, and receiving little back in return. It is no fun being a doormat for others, yet many people go through their entire lives as unpaid servants to their partners. If you are providing emotional support for others, but receiving none back in return, activate this area to create a better balanced relationship.

Maybe your relationship is based solely on physical gratification. There is nothing wrong with this, but it seldom leads to a long-lasting relationship. You can activate this area to become friends as well as bedroom partners.

Anything that is green in color makes a good remedy for this part of your home. Green candles, crystals, potted plants and ornaments all help create harmony and friendship within your home. Make sure that this area is well-lit to encourage the ch'i to flow freely here.

When the Chien area of the home is missing any male occupants will experience problems in getting on with people at work. They are likely to lack motivation and vitality.

Your Love Direction

The eight different directions indicated by the pa-kua all represent different areas of life. In this book, we are concerned only with your love direction. The remaining seven directions are all covered in my book, *Feng Shui for Beginners.*[2]

The trigram that relates to your year of birth also shows your love direction. The directions differ according to your sex.

Love Directions for Men

South: if you were born in 1918, 1927, 1936, 1945, 1954, 1963, 1972, 1980, 1989 or 1998.

North-West: if you were born in 1914, 1917, 1923, 1926, 1932, 1935, 1941, 1944, 1950, 1953, 1959, 1962, 1968, 1971, 1977, 1980, 1986, 1989 or 1995.

South-East: if you were born in 1916, 1925, 1934, 1943, 1952, 1961, 1970, 1979, 1988 or 1997.

East: if you were born in 1915, 1924, 1933, 1942, 1951, 1960, 1969, 1978, 1987 or 1996.

South-West: if you were born in 1913, 1922, 1931, 1940, 1949, 1958, 1967, 1976, 1985 or 1994.

North-East: if you were born in 1912, 1921, 1930, 1939, 1948, 1957, 1966, 1975, 1984 or 1993.

West: if you were born in 1911, 1920, 1929, 1938, 1947, 1956, 1965, 1974, 1983 or 1992.

North: if you were born in 1910, 1919, 1928, 1937, 1946, 1955, 1964, 1973, 1982 or 1991.

Love Directions for Women

South: if you were born in 1914, 1923, 1932, 1941, 1950, 1959, 1968, 1977, 1986 or 1995.

North-West: if you were born in 1915, 1924, 1933, 1942, 1951, 1960, 1969, 1978, 1987 or 1996.

South-East: if you were born in 1916, 1925, 1934, 1943, 1952, 1961, 1970, 1979, 1988 or 1997.

East: if you were born in 1917, 1926, 1935, 1944, 1953, 1962, 1971, 1980, 1989 or 1998.

South-West: if you were born in 1918, 1921, 1927, 1930, 1936, 1939, 1945, 1948, 1954, 1957, 1963, 1966, 1972, 1975, 1981, 1984, 1990 or 1999.

North-East: if you were born in 1919, 1928, 1937, 1946, 1955, 1964, 1973, 1982 or 1991.

West: if you were born in 1911, 1920, 1929, 1938, 1947, 1956, 1965, 1974, 1983 or 1992.

North: if you were born in 1913, 1922, 1931, 1940, 1949, 1958, 1967, 1976, 1985 or 1994.

There is one important exception to the above dates. If you were born in January or the first week of February in any year, you should use the year *before* you were born to determine your love direction. This is because the Chinese calendar does not start on January 1st.

You can use your love direction in a variety of ways. If you can, align your bed so that you sleep facing this direction. Place your favorite chair so that you will sit facing this direction whenever you sit down to relax.

It is unfortunate if your toilet is in this part of your home, as it means that your relationship prospects are being flushed away. Remedy this by keeping the door of the toilet closed at all times, and place a mirror on the outside of the door to symbolically make the room disappear. Do not use this particular toilet, if at all possible.

All of these things need to be considered when looking at your home from a feng shui point of view. Remember that no home is perfect. I have been in homes which are ninety-nine per cent perfect, but have also been in others which were a feng shui nightmare.

Take your time in checking your home. Think carefully about what it is you want your home to provide. Only then start to make changes.

In the next chapter we will see how two people improved their love lives by making changes to their homes.

6

Putting It All Together

You now have all the necessary information to look at your own home and make any necessary changes to improve your love life and happiness.

Over the years, I have performed countless feng shui evaluations of houses, apartments, offices, warehouses, and factories. Usually, my clients are aware that something is not quite right, and call me in to see if feng shui can rectify the problem. I am still trying to find a perfect home. In fact, it would be impossible to find a home that was perfect for everyone. A home that was feng shui perfect for you, might be totally wrong for someone else. As I have yet to find a perfect home, I am invariably able to make suggestions to improve the feng shui and help the occupants. Most people ask for a general consultation. However, an increasing number have been asking for advice on improving their love lives.

Here are two examples to show how feng shui can play a major role in improving this important part of our lives.

The Confirmed Bachelor

John lives on his own in a three-bedroom house in an outer suburb of a large city. He was born in 1954 and had given up hope of ever finding the right relationship. His element is Wood.

"The last serious relationship finished about fifteen years ago," he told me. "It lasted three years. Since then, there have been a few that lasted a week or two, but nothing serious. I try hard, but for some reason I seem to repel all the women I meet!"

John had been living in his present house for exactly fifteen years. He had bought it soon after his last relationship ended. He laughed when I suggested that his house might be affecting his relationships. "I've hardly had a woman in my house since I bought it," he told me.

All the same, he rather skeptically invited me to his home to check it out.

His home was a small, modest-looking bungalow on a street consisting of mainly much larger homes. The front garden was superb. The lawn seemed to have been manicured and the path leading up to the front door was accompanied by beds of brightly colored flowers on both sides. A large cherry tree in the middle of the front lawn provided color and welcome shade. Sometimes a single tree can create a shar, but fortunately this beautiful tree sent no shars towards the house.

I could see the first problem before I even got out of the car. The path leading to the front door was in a straight line from the sidewalk. I received another shock when I reached the front door, as it led directly into a long hallway, creating a continuation of the shar.

John gave me a tour of the house. I was amazed at how tidy and neat everything was. John was obviously an excellent housekeeper.

The living room was extremely large, taking up half of the house. John had it attractively furnished. One corner of this room was used for dining. The kitchen and bathroom were both small, but were well designed and immaculately clean. The three bedrooms were all on the left-hand side of the house. The middle one was used as a guest bedroom, although John ruefully told me that few people had ever slept there. John used the bedroom nearest the front door as a study.

I sketched a plan of the house (Figure 6A) and began by telling him about the shars. I suggested that he either

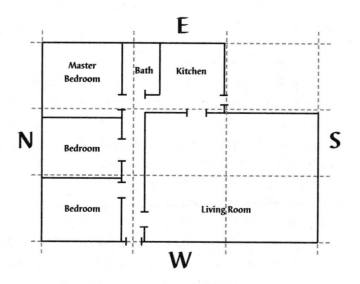

Figure 6A: John's floor plan

rebuild the path leading up to the front door, or place a pa-kua mirror above the front door.

The internal shar, created by the hallway was more serious, as it led directly to the bathroom. This is one room we do not want to be able to see from the front door. In effect, the beneficial ch'i came in through the front door, and raced down the hallway and into the toilet! No wonder John had had problems ever since moving into the house.

Fortunately, because of its position, John kept the bathroom door closed at all times. I suggested that he place a large mirror on the outside of the door to reflect the shar away from the bathroom. I also suggested that he place a mirror on each wall inside the bathroom to symbolically make the room disappear.

I then moved on to look at the house using the Aspirations of the Pa-kua. When I placed the three-by-three magic square over the plan I found that the Marriage sector was completely missing.

"I'm not concerned about marriage," John said. "But I've been like a monk since living here. I just want a girl friend. I've had nothing remotely like a relationship since I moved in."

I suggested that he symbolically finish off the house. There are a number of things he could do here. He could place a lamp in the garden to square off the house. He could build a porch or deck. He could plant flower beds, or he could erect a wall.

I then went through the house, room by room.

The master bedroom was in the Wealth area. The bed was in the corner diagonally across from the entrance, and

John could easily see anyone who came into the room without turning his head. A large window on the East wall allowed direct sunlight on the bed in the morning. This would contribute to John's sleeping problems. I suggested that he keep the curtains pulled on this window until the sun no longer cast direct light on the bed.

The Wealth area is largely wasted as a bedroom, though I suggested he display something relating to his personal element (Wood) in this room to enhance his financial situation. It would have been good to have an aquarium in this room (water creates wood in the productive cycle), but John said he hated fish, and was not prepared to have them, even if they made him a millionaire.

I also suggested that he activate the Marriage sector in this room, by hanging a crystal in the Northeast corner, immediately above a bedside table. I also made the suggestion that he remove the odd items that had been placed on this table and forgotten, as they symbolically represented clutter.

"Put them away where they belong, and only put things on that table that remind you of love and romance. A picture, perhaps."

"Or a small ornament from a childhood sweetheart," John suggested. He opened his wardrobe and produced a small, porcelain ornament of a boy and a girl sitting on a farmyard fence.

"That's perfect!" I exclaimed. "You should display something like that, rather than have it tucked away in a closet."

I watched as John removed the clutter and carefully put the figurine down on the table.

"I've started to feng shui my house!" he said.

The Fame area included most of the bathroom and the kitchen. Water drains away in both of these rooms. This means that symbolically, John's reputation was going down the drain. I suggested that he hang green wind chimes near to the back door to enhance his reputation in the community.

The Family area included most of the second bedroom.

"That's good," John said. The only people who have ever slept there have been relatives and an old school friend."

This room was dark and gloomy. I suggested that he increase the amount of light to encourage more friends into his life. I also suggested that he use the room every now and again. It makes no difference what he does inside the room, just as long as it is used. This symbolically encourages friends to visit.

The Good Luck area took up part of the hallway and almost a quarter of the living room. This is an excellent location for entertaining, but the only item of furniture in this part of the room was a television set. None of the furniture faced in the right direction to comfortably sit and watch the TV.

"How do you watch it?" I asked.

"I lie on the floor," John explained.

"Why is there no other furniture in this part of the room?"

"It would only get in the way of the door to the kitchen," he explained.

"There is any amount of room," I protested. "Try putting a couple of chairs in that part of the room and see what happens."

The Children area took up exactly one-quarter of the living room. John had a dining table and four chairs here. He grinned at me.

"I have no children," he said.

"What do children do?" I asked. "They love to play and have fun. You should activate this area, so that your home becomes full of fun and laughter."

This area was well lit with a large picture-window. I suggested he hang a crystal to capture and hold some of the ch'i.

"Won't that mean my guests will play with their food?" John joked.

"Maybe, but it'll be worth it," I told him. "Try it and see."

The Knowledge area consisted of the third bedroom. Interestingly enough, John used this room as his study. The furniture consisted of a desk and two large bookcases. This room was brighter than the second bedroom as it received afternoon sun. When John sat at his desk, though, his back was to the door.

"Have you heard of people being stabbed in the back?" I asked him.

"You mean office politics? But I'm here all by myself!"

"Of course, but all the same, you'll feel more comfortable if you move the desk so that you can see anyone coming into the room. Even though you know that won't happen."

John looked doubtful. "I'll try it."

I suggested that he hang a crystal in this room to encourage the ch'i in. "You'll find you'll be able to study more effectively that way."

The Career area included part of the front door and hallway, as well as almost a quarter of the living room. John had instinctively placed his telephone and fax machine in this area. I suggested that he also place a potted plant in this area, as it related to his personal element.

Finally, the Mentors area took up the last part of the living room. There were large windows on both exterior walls, providing sunlight here for most of the day. John had a couch against the West wall and an armchair on the South.

"These attract mentors," I told him. "People who can help you."

"That explains why all my visitors are so old!" he said.

"Not necessarily. This area also relates to travel. If you want to travel you should display something that will reflect the light in this area. A crystal, glass ornaments, a mirror perhaps. Something that you find attractive."

"Won't that just attract more old people?"

"Yes and no. Maybe you should rearrange the furniture, so that some of it is in the Good Luck location."

John nodded doubtfully. "There's so much to do."

Usually I suggest that people make just one change at a time and see what happens. In John's case, I suggested he make two changes right away. Obviously, from a relationship point of view the missing Marriage sector had to be corrected first. I also told him to activate the Marriage sector in his bedroom. He had already started on this with the figurine, but as it was important to attract as much ch'i as possible into this location, I suggested that he hang up a crystal right away.

I felt I had done enough for John on this visit. I told him that I'd come back in a month to complete the evaluation using the magic square and the compass directions.

Just two weeks later, John called to say that he had met a charming woman, so it appeared that the feng shui was working. Should he ask her out for a meal, or wait until I had finished the work on his house? I told him to enjoy the dinner.

John appeared transformed when I called on him again. He was much more enthusiastic, and the permanent smile on his face made him appear ten years younger.

"It's working! It's working!" he exclaimed as soon as he opened the door.

I had already worked on the evaluation using the compass directions, so this visit was a simple matter of walking from room to room.

As before, I started with the master bedroom. This room is in the Northeast, which relates to Ken. Ken governs communication, an essential ingredient in any relationship. John admitted that communication had been a major problem in the past.

"I just don't have any small talk," he told me. "I can talk about my work and sport, but I dry up when it's just chit-chat."

The remedy for this is to have something pink or yellow in this part of the house. John balked at the idea of yellow wind chimes in his bedroom, but agreed to buy a yellow ornament to place on top of his wardrobe.

"Remember that communication can take a number of forms," I told him. "You may find that something yellow in this room will increase all types of communication."

We then went through to the kitchen.

"This area, and the bathroom, relate to Chen," I told him. "This represents outside influences. Unfortunately, they are usually negative, rather than positive."

"Someone at work was telling me not to get myself too involved too quickly," John said. "Is that the sort of thing you mean?"

"Exactly. That person probably means well, and has your best interests at heart, but isn't helping. We're all influenced to a certain extent by others. Goodness knows how many potentially good relationships have been broken up by outside interference."

I suggested that John display items in the kitchen and bathroom that made him feel good. He already had a drawing of a heart attached to the refrigerator door with a magnet. "My niece drew that for me," John said. "It makes me smile every time I see it."

"That's perfect feng shui," I told him. "That picture is generating good ch'i for you."

Calm, peaceful colors also make a good cure in this location. John's bathroom decor was an extremely pale blue, which served as a good remedy.

We then went out the backdoor and looked at the piece of land that represented the missing area of his house.

"This area is known as Sun," I told him. "It relates to love, harmony and happiness. Unfortunately, this is missing from your home."

"I'm going to finish it off with a lamp in the garden," John told me. "You suggested that last month and I've been thinking about it a lot."

"That's good. You could also hang wind chimes to help activate love and happiness. You certainly need to finish off this corner in some way, as when the Sun area is missing you are likely to have bad luck and disappointments."

John grimaced. "I've had enough of those. I should have done something about this long ago."

We retraced our steps through the kitchen and went to the second bedroom. This room relates to K'an, which helps relationships to move forward and to develop.

"That's what I need," John said. "What can I do in here to help that?"

"You need something that is red or pink. Plants would be good, but this is the coldest, darkest room in the house, so artificial plants would probably be better than live ones. You'll have to look after them well, though, whether they're alive or artificial. A hanging mobile that was red or green would be good. A piece of rose quartz will also help. Also, keep this room as well lit as you can to encourage the ch'i in. Use the room, too. All of these things will help your relationship progress, and they'll all help physical passion as well."

John smiled as he wrote down my suggestions.

We went through to the third bedroom, saving the living room until last.

"This room relates to Chien," I said. "From your point of view, this is one of the most important rooms in the house. If you want a partner who is both a lover and a friend, you should activate this area. If you do this, you'll also attract more friends of both sexes into your life."

John nodded. "Sounds good to me. What do I do?"

"You need some green in this room. Maybe a potted plant, a candle or ornament."

"What say I paint the cupboard door green?"

I nodded. "That would definitely help. In fact, it would give you all the green you'd need. Alternatively, you could have a number of green items in the room. You could buy green pens, for instance, to keep on your desk. Anything green, anything at all, just as long as you find it attractive."

I had saved the living room as last, as it was a large room that incorporated four different areas. It is not good to have a room that is so disproportionally large, compared to the rest of the house, as it is inclined to dominate the home. We stood in the Good Luck Center and looked around.

"This room's feeling better," I commented.

John nodded. "I've added two lights," he told me. "I'm also letting more fresh air in when I'm home. I've noticed a difference in here, too. It feels so much more comfortable. Like a home, really. It's funny when you think about it, but I've never considered this house to be home until now. I was skeptical, I must admit, but the ch'i is certainly helping me."

As well as the Good Luck Center, John's living room also contained Li in the South, Tui in the West and K'un in the Southwest. The sun was coming through the windows on the south wall, lighting up the Li area.

"It's good to have all that sunlight in that part of the room," I commented. "As well as activating the ch'i, it also activates your sex life. Actually, you probably don't need to do anything in this part of the room. However, if that area needs stimulating, put something red in the Li part of the room. By the way, this direction—South—is known as your love direction, and it's good to see it activated in this way."

"Hmm." John nodded his head. "Are you sure a bit more red will get my love life going again? Right! This part of the room will be really well activated!"

"Over in the corner is the K'un area," I continued. This relates largely to our feelings. You should activate this part of the room when you find it hard to express your inner-most feelings."

John nodded again. "I badly need help in that area."

"Okay. Try displaying some ceramic or pottery orna-ments in this part of the room. Crystals would be good, as well. Once you find yourself in a stable relationship, this would be the perfect place to display photographs of the two of you."

John turned to face the Tui area of the room. "What should I do here?"

"This area relates to passion. If you're lacking in that area, and I guess you probably are from what you've told me, you need to activate this part of the room. Flowers and plants will do that wonderfully well. Coincidentally, they also relate to your element. It would be good to also have something here that included Water, as Water comes immediately before Wood in the productive cycle of ele-ments."

"Like a small fountain?"

"Yes. And I know you don't like aquariums, but this would also be a good place for a fish bowl of some sort."

"I want the passion, not the fish!"

"You can increase the passion by having red objects in this area. A red candle is ideal, as it symbolizes the flame of passion burning brightly. It's also highly romantic, if you're entertaining someone in this room."

John looked around, a slight smile on his face.

"I think I have a red candle," he mused.

John gradually made a series of adjustments to his home. Once he started getting results, he wanted to speed up the process and do everything all at once. However, I insisted he make the changes gradually.

He is not married yet, but his current relationship has lasted more than a year. Jacqui has been living with him for the last nine months, and they seem to be extremely happy.

The Unhappy Widow

I met Maureen after a talk I gave on feng shui for singles. She was an attractive businesswoman who carried an air of sadness around with her like an aura. She was a friend of the organizer of the event and joined us for a coffee once the evening was over.

Maureen was born on November 22nd, 1966, which meant that her element was Fire. Her husband had been killed in a car accident three years before, just one day short of their fifth wedding anniversary. She had known him since she was sixteen and was still finding it hard to face life without him.

"Yes, I do want to get married again," she told me. "I realize no one can replace my Kevin, but I think I'm ready to start dating again."

Maureen had had plenty of suitors in her three years of widowhood, but she had turned them all down as she was still grieving. She wanted to know what she could do to her apartment to encourage love into her life again.

Maureen had a small apartment on the ground floor of an attractive apartment complex overlooking a small lake. The situation was superb, and she could sit in her living room and enjoy looking out at the park and water views (see Figure 6B).

A winding path led to her front door. She had a flower garden on each side of the path, creating an abundance of ch'i. Unfortunately, though, the back door was directly

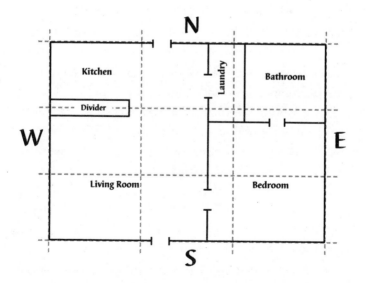

Figure 6B: Maureen's floor plan

opposite the front door, which meant that the ch'i came into the apartment, and raced through the living room and kitchen and out the back door.

The living room and kitchen were actually one room, with a room divider that acted as a counter separating the two areas. This meant that there was not enough room to put up a screen to hide the back door from view. I suggested that she hang a crystal from the ceiling midway between the front and back doors to act as a remedy.

The apartment had one bedroom, and the bathroom led off from it. Maureen had always felt awkward inviting friends to visit as she did not like them having to go through her bedroom to use the bathroom.

I could understand Maureen's concern about this. However, the main feng shui problem with this arrangement was that negative, or shar-ch'i, would come into her bedroom from the bathroom. Fortunately, she kept the bathroom door closed all the time, which acted as a partial remedy. I suggested that she place a small round mirror on the bedroom side of this door to symbolically make the room disappear. Normally, I would suggest a large mirror on the outside of this door, but this would have reflected Maureen's bed, solving one problem but creating another.

Apart from these difficulties, the apartment was ideal for her needs. The front door faced South, and her bedroom and living room received sunlight all day long. Consequently, the apartment was always pleasantly warm, even in winter.

As I had with John, I began by doing an assessment using the Aspirations of the Pa-kua.

The Wealth area took up two thirds of the kitchen.

"Unfortunately, this means that your wealth is going down the drain," I told Maureen.

She nodded. "That figures. I haven't saved a cent since I've been here."

I suggested that she keep this part of the room well-lit to attract more ch'i into the kitchen area. I also suggested that she might like to have some plants on the window ledge.

The Fame area consisted of the rest of the kitchen and most of the laundry. This part of the kitchen was dead space with nothing in it. The laundry contained a pile of unwashed clothes and sheets.

"As I live on my own, I wait until I have a decent load to put through," Maureen explained.

Unfortunately, this pile of laundry created clutter. I explained what this meant this to Maureen.

"You should keep the door closed to hide the clutter," I said. "Also, if you want to improve your standing or reputation, you should do something about this area."

"It's really just my love life I'm interested in at the moment," she said.

I took her through to the bathroom. "This is the Marriage or relationship area," I told her.

She shook her head. "Are you telling me my love life is going down the toilet?"

"In a sense. You'll have to pay particular attention to this area to encourage romance."

"What should I do?"

Her eagerness made me laugh. "Unfortunately, this is the gloomiest room in the house. You need much more light in here."

"Crystals! Should I have crystals in here?"

"They'd certainly help," I agreed. "You also need a few things in here that remind you of love and romance."

Maureen had a laminated poster of a Valentine's Day heart that someone had given her two years earlier. It had been stored under her bed, as she thought she had nowhere suitable to hang it. Before I left, it was proudly displayed in the bathroom.

"Whenever you see it, it will remind you of love," I said.

"Like an affirmation?"

"That's right. But it's more than that, as it will actually attract love to you."

Maureen grinned. "I can hardly wait!"

The Family and friends area took up a third of the living area, and Maureen had a comfortable settee against the West wall where her visitors usually sat. This location is known as the power position, because her visitors were able to see the front door without turning their heads.

The Good Luck Center was largely wasted in the living room. A bookcase on the wall revealed Maureen's interests in music and theater, but there was no room for other furniture as it would restrict access to the kitchen area. Fortunately, the crystal that I suggested as a remedy for the straight line between the front and back doors would also help activate the Good Luck Center.

"Good. I could do with some luck," Maureen said.

The Children area took up a third of the bedroom and a small part of the laundry and bathroom.

"It's a good thing my bed's not in this part of the room," Maureen commented. "The last thing I want is children."

"It relates to young people generally," I told her. "Incidentally, it's reasonably well activated by the light coming in through the windows."

The Knowledge area took up a quarter of the living room. Maureen had a large armchair in this location.

"I curl up in it and read and read and read," she told me.

The Career area was immediately inside the front door, and also took up a small part of the bedroom. A small side table just inside the front door held Maureen's fax machine and telephone.

"I used to hate it being there," she said. "But for some reason I never got around to moving it. I must have procrastinated intuitively!"

Finally, we returned to the bedroom to look at the Mentors area. Most of this was taken up with Maureen's double bed.

"I've had no mentors in there," she laughed. "Sad to say, I'm the only person who ever uses this area."

I then explained how the Aspirations could be used for individual rooms.

"This means that your bed is in the Marriage sector of the room. You could activate this area to further help you attract love."

"There's no room to do anything."

On the South wall beside the bed Maureen had several photographs of her and her late husband. She saw me looking at them.

"I couldn't take them down," she said.

"They would be better in your living room," I said. "They're important to you, of course, and should be displayed. Unfortunately, though, they hinder the potential of a new relationship where they are now. What you should do is use that wall to display something that you consider romantic."

Maureen took them down while I used a compass to determine the direction the house faced.

"This is a K'an house," I told her. "It sits to the North and the front door faces South. There are four positive and four negative directions in every home. We'll go through the house in the same order as before." I led the way through to the kitchen. "This area is ruled by Chien and represents friendship. You need to pay special attention to this area if you find yourself too busy to enjoy happy times with your friends."

Maureen laughed. "Sounds like me. What should I do in here?"

"I've already suggested some live plants, but you could also use anything else that is green in color. Green is a relaxing, peaceful color and will help you enjoy happy times with your friends. It could even open the door to finding the right person for you."

"Okay." Maureen nodded. "I'll do it. What about the back door?"

"That area, plus most of the laundry, relates to K'an. This is a special area that will help you get going again. If you activate this area, you'll find it much easier to get motivated to find the right relationship."

"Or any relationship!"

"Initially. Ultimately, though, it will help attract the perfect person to you."

"What do I do?"

"I'd hang up a wind chime near the back door. Use a metal wind chime that is red or pink. Whenever you hear it, it will remind you that the ch'i is flowing. I'd also get a piece of rose quartz and display it in the laundry. It would also be a good idea to increase the light just inside the back door. The rest of the kitchen is fine, but it looks a bit gloomy by the door. Extra light will attract more ch'i."

We went through to Maureen's bathroom.

"This area relates to Ken. Ken relates to communication."

"But I'm on my own. I don't speak to anyone, except on the phone."

"Try activating this area, and you'll find more people to communicate with."

Maureen frowned. "I've always discouraged visitors," she said. She indicated the bathroom. "Because of this room, really."

Maureen's bathroom was spotlessly clean. The main color was pink, though she had a blue bathmat on the floor.

"Try using a bit of yellow in this room," I suggested. "Yellow encourages communication. Yellow bath towels would work well in here. I know you don't like taking people through your bedroom to the bathroom, but by the time we are finished, that shouldn't be a problem."

We went back to the living area and stood by the divider that separated this area from the kitchen.

"This part of the room relates to sensuality. It is connected to the Tui trigram in feng shui. Incidentally, West is your love direction."

"The only thing I'm missing is a partner!" Maureen said wistfully.

"What you need in this area is anything from the Wood element," I told her. This is because her personal element is Fire, and she needed something from the element that preceded hers to activate this area. "Flowers, or potted plants, perhaps. You could even have artificial flowers, if you were too busy to look after live ones. As it also represents your love direction, you should have freshly cut flowers that remind you of love and romance. It doesn't matter if you buy them yourself, by the way. Also, hang up a few things in this area that remind you of love."

We moved into the spiritual center of the apartment.

"You should sit here to relax and think about the sort of relationship you want. I realize there is not much room for a chair, but you could always pull that armchair over whenever you are doing this." I laughed at the expression on Maureen's face. "Try it and see for yourself."

We went back into her bedroom and I indicated the area occupied by Chen (a quarter of the bedroom and part of the bathroom).

"This relates to outside influences," I told her. "People who try to help you find a relationship, perhaps, but really aren't helping."

"That sounds like just about everyone at work!"

"Display things that are peaceful here. Anything that is calming or soothing would do. I see that you like crystals, so aquamarine would work well here."

We returned to the living room and looked at the Southwest part of the room.

"This area is known as K'un and relates to your feelings. It enjoys plenty of sunlight, which attracts a great deal of ch'i. Consequently, this area is just about perfect, unless you are having problems with your feelings."

Maureen shook her head. "I don't think I have too many problems there."

"That's good. I normally suggest that people display something red in this area if they are having problems in that regard. By the way, this would be a good place to display the photographs you have in your bedroom."

We moved a few steps to stand just inside the front door.

"This area relates to Li. It represents closeness and your sex life. You should display something red in color here, as it will draw people to you."

"I'll do that today!"

"We have just one area left," I said as we returned to Maureen's bedroom and looked at the area occupied by her double bed. This area is called Sun and relates to happiness. Fortunately, this area is well lit, which means that the ch'i is attracted to it."

"I guess I'm reasonably happy. I've been on my own a bit too long, I think. Apart from that, I guess I'm happy again. I've never stopped to think about it in those terms."

"A bit of green here would make you even happier. Green relates to the element that precedes yours, so will help attract peace, contentment and even love."

"I have a green bedspread that I've never used."

"Get it out," I suggested. "Try it and see what happens."

As always, I suggested that Maureen make just one change at a time. She was too impatient to do that, and when I saw her again several weeks later, she had made all the changes I suggested.

"What does your home feel like now?" I asked.

"Wonderful! I feel poised and ready to start my life again."

I did not see Maureen again for eighteen months. She was sitting in the front row at a talk I gave. The man sitting beside her had his arm protectively around her shoulders. They both looked very happy.

7

Improving Existing Relationships

Sad to say, passion does not always last forever. Many couples who enjoyed a happy, stimulating love life in the early years of their relationship find that the passion gradually fades and intercourse becomes a rare occurrence. This is not a problem if both people are happy with the lack of intimacy. However, this situation can easily destroy a once happy relationship if one person wants to make love regularly and the other does not. Fortunately, there are a number of feng shui remedies that can be used to stimulate and revitalize tired relationships.

Most people feel that everyone else is enjoying a better sex life than they are. However, many people lie about their sex lives. One famous author I knew continually boasted about his sex life. After he died, his past wives admitted that he been impotent for many years and his sex life had been non-existent.

Consequently, it pays to ignore most of what other people tell you about this subject. Two friends of mine talk about the subject in different ways. One tells everyone that even after twenty years of marriage, he and his wife still make love five or six times a week. The other one talks about the "annual event." For all I know, both could be lying and the one who says he makes love once a year may well be enjoying it every night, while the other one is celibate.

The message is simple. If you feel that your sex life is fine, it is. It makes no difference how frequently or infrequently you and your partner make love, just as long as you are both happy with the situation. However, this chapter is for people who are not happy with their current situation.

If your relationship is good in most respects, but is lacking passion between the sheets, there are a number of feng shui things that you can do.

Obviously, the first area to look at is the marriage area in your home. Is there clutter here? Is it dark and gloomy? Is it hard for the ch'i to find this area?

Activate this area with anything that represents love and romance to you. Increase the amount of light to encourage the ch'i in. Increase the amount of red in the color scheme.

Do the same in the marriage sector of your bedroom. You may have to carefully monitor the amount of red you use.

One lady I know bought red sheets and immediately found that her husband, who normally fell asleep as soon as his head hit the pillow, suddenly wanted to make love all the time.

"I almost died from lack of sleep," she told me. "I have a responsible job and three children to look after. I need my rest!"

Carefully examine the placement of any mirrors in the bedroom. It is impossible to have too many mirrors from a feng shui point of view, but they need to be placed extremely carefully in the bedroom. Any mirrors that reflect you and your partner in bed symbolically represent other people intruding into the relationship. At almost every talk I give, someone jokingly mentions a mirror in the ceiling above the bed. This probably works extremely well for short-term, highly passionate relationships, but is disastrous for long-term relationships.

Many people experience marital problems shortly after moving house, or after major renovations to their home. When this happens, you can virtually guarantee that there is a problem with the feng shui. In this case, you should evaluate the entire house, beginning with the front door. The problem is usually to be found in the bedroom, but it is a mistake to assume that this will always be the case. You should examine each part of the house in turn to see if you can uncover any feng shui problems.

If you have undergone a major redecoration in your home, you might assume that the problem will be in the areas that have been changed. However, this may not be correct. Something in the new or altered area might be casting a shar on an area that has not been changed.

You might be in a situation where your love life is fine, but the two of you still seem to have drifted apart with little or no real communication going on. This is a danger sign. No matter how good the sex is, you still need communication and companionship.

The remedy for this is to bring something yellow into the marriage area of your home, and into this part of your bedroom. Yellow represents communication. Be careful not to overdo it, as too much yellow can cause headaches.

Yellow is a stimulating color and you are likely to find yourself doing more things together than ever before. A friend told me that she had seen more movies in the twelve months since she had introduced some yellow cushions into her home, than she had seen in the previous twenty years. She also happily told me that she and her husband were communicating well, and that every other aspect of their lives was going well also.

Work can sometimes drive couples apart. If someone is working extremely hard, maybe spending long hours at the office, or bringing work home each night, the other partner can feel neglected. This is especially the case if the person doing all the hard work is constantly tired or stressed. There may not be anything you can do about the volume of work, but you can keep your love life active by introducing a small amount of red into the bedroom. I wonder if John Milton knew all about this when he wrote these lines in *Paradise Lost*: "With a smile that glowed Celestial rosy red, love's proper hue."[1]

It is also a good idea to place a pair of ornaments in the area where the person sits or works at home. Traditionally, the remedy has always been two mandarin ducks, but a pair of anything will work wonders. Two ducks, or two dogs, lions, fish, or anything else, represent both partners in the marriage and help stimulate the relationship.

Remember the yin and yang aspects of relationships. When yang increases, yin decreases, and vice versa. If one partner is trying to be totally yang, for instance, and acts in a macho, aggressive, determined, and emotionless way there are bound to be problems. However, this situation cannot last for long, as when yang reaches its full height, yin starts to come in to create equilibrium again. People who try to express only the yin or only the yang sides of their natures are doomed to confusion, frustration, and ultimately loneliness.

It is just as destructive to try being totally yin. We all have elements of both yin and yang in our makeup, and to try to deny one of these is unhealthy and dangerous.

Ultimately, you should be what you are, and not try to be what you are not. You should look at your partner dispassionately and decide if he or she is predominantly yin or yang. This has nothing to do with the person's sexuality. Then look at yourself and decide if you are more yin than yang, or the other way around. Looking at your selves in this way can be extremely revealing, and will help both of you to balance and harmonize your relationship. This leads to deeper understanding and will bring you closer together.

Finally, if you are having problems, sit down and talk. Feng shui can help resolve difficulties, but it can not do it on its own. You may have to leave the house and talk quietly in a park or restaurant. It is often easier to have serious discussions of this sort away from your home environment. Talking over your problems in this way is a sign that you both want the relationship to continue. No matter how old you are, if you have love and goodwill on both sides, plus feng shui, you can enhance your existing relationship and make it better than ever been before.

8

Feng Shui for Companionship

Not everyone wants a lover, but we all need friends. I am frequently asked at my lectures if feng shui can be used to attract friends, who may or may not ever become lovers. The answer is "yes."

Another question I am asked, usually immediately after the first one, is if it is possible for a man and a woman to become good friends, in a relationship that has no sexual connotations or overtones. Again, the answer is "yes." I have a number of good female friends and thoroughly enjoy their company, and assume that they also enjoy spending time with me. Naturally, there is a yin and a yang element involved in these friendships, but this is good as we all benefit from spending time with people of the opposite sex.

Many of the people who ask these questions are elderly. They want to spend time with people of the opposite sex, but have no desire for anything other than friendship. Fortunately, feng shui can be extremely useful in this regard.

The first thing to do is to use the Aspirations of the Pakua and examine the Family area of your home. This area is related to good friends and health, as well as the immediate family. Naturally, you should increase the amount of light in this area. A large mirror will give feelings of expansiveness and encourage visitors. Objects belonging to your personal element (or the element preceding yours in the productive cycle) will also help activate this location.

Next, you must ensure that all the chairs and couches are being used. Many people living on their own habitually use just one or two chairs in the house. This discourages visitors. Use all the chairs in rotation and you will quickly notice a difference. It is particularly important to use all the chairs around the dining room table, as this is related to abundance in every sense of the word.

Finally, pay attention to the entrance of your home. Is it well-lit and inviting? You want to encourage the ch'i in through the front door. If the ch'i comes in readily, so will your visitors.

There are two other factors that are important to people living on their own: low self-esteem and fear. Many people on their own become inward-looking and introspective because of the long hours they spend in their own company. During this time many of them think negative thoughts about themselves, and these ultimately affect their self-esteem and confidence. Consequently, when they do emerge from their homes, they subconsciously discourage potential friendships by being too self-contained. If you have been on your own for a long while you may have to force yourself to be more outgoing and friendly.

Fear is an even greater problem. People who have been hurt in the past are often reluctant to try again. It is easier to stay at home, feeling sorry for yourself, than it is to go out and risk rejection.

An acquaintance of mine went through a particularly difficult and painful divorce about twelve years ago. He is still suffering as a result of this, and consequently seldom goes anywhere where he can meet women. He is a kind, gentle man, but he has put a hard, bitter, cynical screen around himself which ensures that he will never find another partner. Basically, he is still hurting and is terrified that any new relationship will end in the same way his marriage did. This means that he is caught in an insidious trap. Until he releases this screen he will not meet anyone. But releasing the screen means that he might get hurt again. He is aware of this, and is becoming more embittered all the time because of the situation he is in. Fear is stopping him from allowing the real person to emerge, and is also preventing him from finding a good, loving relationship.

Many elderly people also suffer from fear. Almost every day we read in the newspapers about elderly people being beaten up or taken advantage of in some way. It is no wonder that so many elderly people lead lonely lives, inside a prison of their own making.

There are, however, many activities available for the elderly, providing opportunities for companionship and friendship. If they can let go of their fear, and take advantage of these opportunities, life can become so much more enjoyable. An eighty-one year old friend of mine has recently taken up ballroom dancing and is having a wonderful time.

"There are three women for every man," he told me. "I should have taken this up years ago!"

My friend had had many lonely years before taking up dancing. He had to force himself out of his comfort zone, something he found extremely hard to do as he had become set in his ways. Once he had done it, though, he could not believe the change in his life.

If you have been living on your own for too long, think carefully about what you would like to do, and then make the first step. There are countless people out there who would love to get to know you. They cannot do this if you are sitting all alone in your apartment.

Last year I did a series of talks for a singles association. I could not believe the large numbers of attractive people of all ages who came to hear what I, and the other speakers, had to say. Although we were the catalyst that encouraged people to come to the meetings, the real purpose was to enable the registrants to meet others.

There are a large number of lonely people out there. If you are one of them, take the first step. Activate the Friends section of your home, and then force yourself to go out and meet people. Go to places and activities that interest you. You will meet like-minded people there. Be open and friendly. Be cautious, too, of course. Take your time, and see what develops. There is no need to be lonely. Be a friend to others and you will soon find yourself more popular than ever before.

Conclusion

I hope this book will either help you find the right partner, or greatly improve your existing relationship. Remember, that in feng shui it is better to make one small change at a time. This gives you an opportunity to evaluate the results of every change you make. It is a natural human desire to rush in and make all the changes at once. However, when you do it this way, you can not determine which changes were beneficial and which were not. Also, in your haste, you might actually do more harm than good.

It is better to make just one small step at a time, wait a few weeks and assess the results, and then make another small change. It might take a little bit longer to attract the right partner or to revitalize your existing relationship by taking one step at a time, but the final result will bring great joy and happiness into your life.

My parents were keen readers and frequently told me interesting quotes that they had read. Two of my mother's favorites were by Victor Hugo who wrote: "The greatest happiness of life is the conviction that we are loved, loved for ourselves, or rather, loved in spite of ourselves." He also wrote: "Life is a flower of which love is the honey."

My father often quoted Sir William Temple's famous words: "The greatest pleasure of life is love."

I hope this book helps you find the greatest pleasure of life.

Appendix

Elements and Signs for the Years 1900 to 2000

Element	Sign	Year
Metal	Rat	Jan. 31, 1900 to Feb. 18, 1901
Metal	Ox	Feb. 19, 1901 to Feb. 7, 1902
Water	Tiger	Feb. 8, 1902 to Jan. 28, 1903
Water	Rabbit	Jan. 29, 1903 to Feb. 15, 1904
Wood	Dragon	Feb. 16, 1904 to Feb. 3, 1905
Wood	Snake	Feb. 4, 1905 to Jan. 24, 1906
Fire	Horse	Jan. 25, 1906 to Feb. 12, 1907
Fire	Sheep	Feb. 13, 1907 to Feb. 1, 1908
Earth	Monkey	Feb. 2, 1908 to Jan. 21, 1909
Earth	Rooster	Jan. 22, 1909 to Feb. 9, 1910
Metal	Dog	Feb. 10, 1910 to Jan. 29, 1911
Metal	Boar	Jan. 30, 1911 to Feb. 17, 1912
Water	Rat	Feb. 18, 1912 to Feb. 5, 1913
Water	Ox	Feb. 6, 1913 to Jan. 25, 1914
Wood	Tiger	Jan. 26, 1914 to Feb. 13, 1915

Wood	Rabbit	Feb. 14, 1915 to Feb. 2, 1916
Fire	Dragon	Feb. 3, 1916 to Jan. 22, 1917
Fire	Snake	Jan. 23, 1917 to Feb. 10, 1918
Earth	Horse	Feb. 11, 1918 to Jan. 31, 1919
Earth	Sheep	Feb. 1, 1919 to Feb. 19, 1920
Metal	Monkey	Feb. 20, 1920 to Feb. 7, 1921
Metal	Rooster	Feb. 8, 1921 to Jan. 27, 1922
Water	Dog	Jan. 28, 1922 to Feb. 15, 1923
Water	Boar	Feb. 16, 1923 to Feb. 4, 1924
Wood	Rat	Feb. 5, 1924 to Jan. 24, 1925
Wood	Ox	Jan. 25, 1925 to Feb. 12, 1926
Fire	Tiger	Feb. 13, 1926 to Feb. 1, 1927
Fire	Rabbit	Feb. 2, 1927 to Jan. 22, 1928
Earth	Dragon	Jan. 23, 1928 to Feb. 9, 1929
Earth	Snake	Feb. 10, 1929 to Jan. 29, 1930
Metal	Horse	Jan. 30, 1930 to Feb. 16, 1931
Metal	Sheep	Feb. 17, 1931 to Feb. 5, 1932
Water	Monkey	Feb. 6, 1932 to Jan. 25, 1933
Water	Rooster	Jan. 26, 1933 to Feb. 13, 1934
Wood	Dog	Feb. 14, 1934 to Feb. 3, 1935
Wood	Boar	Feb. 4, 1935 to Jan. 23, 1936
Fire	Rat	Jan. 24, 1936 to Feb. 10, 1937
Fire	Ox	Feb. 11, 1937 to Jan. 30, 1938
Earth	Tiger	Jan. 31, 1938 to Feb. 18, 1939
Earth	Rabbit	Feb. 19, 1939 to Feb. 7, 1940
Metal	Dragon	Feb. 8, 1940 to Jan. 26, 1941
Metal	Snake	Jan. 27, 1941 to Feb. 14, 1942
Water	Horse	Feb. 15, 1942 to Feb. 4, 1943
Water	Sheep	Feb. 5, 1943 to Jan. 24, 1944
Wood	Monkey	Jan. 25, 1944 to Feb. 12, 1945

Wood	Rooster	Feb. 13, 1945 to Feb. 1, 1946
Fire	Dog	Feb. 2, 1946 to Jan. 21, 1947
Fire	Boar	Jan. 22, 1947 to Feb. 9, 1948
Earth	Rat	Feb. 10, 1948 to Jan. 28, 1949
Earth	Ox	Jan. 29, 1949 to Feb. 16, 1950
Metal	Tiger	Feb. 17, 1950 to Feb. 5, 1951
Metal	Rabbit	Feb. 6, 1951 to Jan. 26, 1952
Water	Dragon	Jan. 27, 1952 to Feb. 13, 1953
Water	Snake	Feb. 14, 1953 to Feb. 2, 1954
Wood	Horse	Feb. 3, 1954 to Jan. 23, 1955
Wood	Sheep	Jan. 24, 1955 to Feb. 11, 1956
Fire	Monkey	Feb. 12, 1956 to Jan. 30, 1957
Fire	Rooster	Jan. 31, 1957 to Feb. 17, 1958
Earth	Dog	Feb. 18, 1958 to Feb. 7, 1959
Earth	Boar	Feb. 8, 1959 to Jan. 27, 1960
Metal	Rat	Jan. 28, 1960 to Feb. 14, 1961
Metal	Ox	Feb. 15, 1961 to Feb. 4, 1962
Water	Tiger	Feb. 5, 1962 to Jan. 24, 1963
Water	Rabbit	Jan. 25, 1963 to Feb. 12, 1964
Wood	Dragon	Feb. 13, 1964 to Feb. 1, 1965
Wood	Snake	Feb. 2, 1965 to Jan. 20, 1966
Fire	Horse	Jan. 21, 1966 to Feb. 8, 1967
Fire	Sheep	Feb. 9, 1967 to Jan. 29, 1968
Earth	Monkey	Jan. 30, 1968 to Feb. 16, 1969
Earth	Rooster	Feb. 17, 1969 to Feb. 5, 1970
Metal	Dog	Feb. 6, 1970 to Jan. 26, 1971
Metal	Boar	Jan. 27, 1971 to Jan. 15, 1972
Water	Rat	Jan. 16, 1972 to Feb. 2, 1973
Water	Ox	Feb. 3, 1973 to Jan. 22, 1974
Wood	Tiger	Jan. 23, 1974 to Feb. 10, 1975

Wood	Rabbit	Feb. 11, 1975 to Jan. 30, 1976
Fire	Dragon	Jan. 31, 1976 to Feb. 17, 1977
Fire	Snake	Feb. 18, 1977 to Feb. 6, 1978
Earth	Horse	Feb. 7, 1978 to Jan. 27, 1979
Earth	Sheep	Jan. 28, 1979 to Feb. 15, 1980
Metal	Monkey	Feb. 16, 1980 to Feb. 4, 1981
Metal	Rooster	Feb. 5, 1981 to Jan. 24, 1982
Water	Dog	Jan. 25, 1982 to Feb. 12, 1983
Water	Boar	Feb. 13, 1983 to Feb. 1, 1984
Wood	Rat	Feb. 2, 1984 to Feb. 19, 1985
Wood	Ox	Feb. 20, 1985 to Feb. 8, 1986
Fire	Tiger	Feb. 9, 1986 to Jan. 28, 1987
Fire	Rabbit	Jan. 29, 1987 to Feb. 16, 1988
Earth	Dragon	Feb. 17, 1988 to Feb. 5, 1989
Earth	Snake	Feb. 6, 1989 to Jan. 26, 1990
Metal	Horse	Jan. 27, 1990 to Feb. 14, 1991
Metal	Sheep	Feb. 15, 1991 to Feb. 3, 1992
Water	Monkey	Feb. 4, 1992 to Jan. 22, 1993
Water	Rooster	Jan. 23, 1993 to Feb. 9, 1994
Wood	Dog	Feb. 10, 1994 to Jan. 30, 1995
Wood	Boar	Jan. 31, 1995 to Feb. 18, 1996
Fire	Rat	Feb. 19, 1996 to Feb. 6, 1997
Fire	Ox	Feb. 7, 1997 to Jan. 27, 1998
Earth	Tiger	Jan. 28, 1998 to Feb. 15, 1999
Earth	Rabbit	Feb. 16, 1999 to Feb. 4, 2000
Metal	Dragon	Feb. 5, 2000

Notes

Introduction

1. James J. Lynch, *The Broken Heart: The Medical Consequences of Loneliness* (New York: Basic Books, Inc., 1977), page 69.

2. James J. Lynch, *The Broken Heart: The Medical Consequences of Loneliness,* page 69.

3. John and Agnes Sturt, *Created for Intimacy* (Guildford, Surrey: Eagle, 1996), pages 9–10.

4. Laurence Turner, *People-Watching* (Ottawa, New Vision, 1992), page 112.

5. Cliff Richard, *Single-Minded* (London: Hodder and Stoughton Limited, 1988), page 79.

6. Dr. Peter Marsh (editor), *Eye to Eye: Your Relationships and How They Work* (London: Sidgwick and Jackson, 1988), page 135.

7. Dr. Peter Marsh (editor), *Eye to Eye: Your Relationships and How They Work,* page 134.

8. The Holy Bible, *Song of Solomon,* 5:16. Quote taken from the King James version.

Chapter One

1. Richard Webster, *Dowsing for Beginners* (St. Paul, MN: Llewellyn Publications, 1996), 110–113. The only shar that cannot be remedied occurs when your house is situated directly beneath high tension power lines. There is increasing evidence that links these overhead power lines to a variety of illnesses. It is also difficult to remedy underground streams. The most effective remedy is to move house.

2. Martin Palmer, *Yin and Yang* (London: Judy Piatkus (Publishers) Limited, 1997), page 14.

3. Wei Tsuei, *Roots of Chinese Culture and Medicine* (Selangor, Malaysia: Pelanduk Publications (M) Sdn. Bhd., 1992), pages 71–84.

4. Louis Culling, *The Pristine Yi King* (St. Paul, MN: Llewellyn Publications, 1989), page 70.

5. Martin Palmer, *Yin and Yang,* page 69.

6. Richard Webster, *Omens, Oghams and Oracles* (St. Paul, MN: Llewellyn Publications, 1995), 10–20.

7. Albert Low, *Feng Shui: The Way to Harmony* (Selangor, Malaysia: Pelanduk Publications (M) Sdn. Bhd., 1993), page 114.

Chapter Five

1. Richard Webster, *Feng Shui for Beginners* (St. Paul, MN: Llewellyn Publications, 1997), 91–94.
2. Richard Webster, *Feng Shui for Beginners*, pages 45–75.

Chapter Seven

1. John Milton, *Paradise Lost,* 1:618. There are numerous versions of this work. Mine is: *Paradise Lost and Paradise Regained* by John Milton (Chicago, IL: Mayne Editions, 1963), 124.

Glossary

Aspirations of the Pa-kua — The Aspirations of the Pa-Kua is controversial, as it is related to the Compass School, but does not use the directions of the compass. It uses the nine boxes created from the magic square found on the back of a tortoise by Wu of Hsia and aligns them over the floor plan of a house (or room, or even a desk), using the position of the main entrance to determine how it is placed.

Ch'i — Ch'i is the universal life force that is found in all living things. In feng shui we want to attract as much ch'i as possible into our homes and work environments. Ch'i is created all the time in nature, and is also created when anything is done perfectly. For example, a sculptor creating a magnificent figure out of a piece of marble is also creating ch'i.

Clutter — Clutter is anything that impedes the smooth flow of ch'i as it spreads throughout the house. Many people find it hard to get rid of belongings that are no longer needed, and these all constitute clutter. It is important to keep our homes as free of clutter as possible as it constricts and limits the beneficial ch'i, consequently holding us back from attaining our dreams and goals.

Compass School — The Compass School is a branch of feng shui that uses the eight compass directions, along with the person's date of birth, to determine the best locations and directions for the person.

Cures — See **Remedies**

Destructive Cycle — The destructive cycle is an arrangement of the five elements that has each one symbolically destroying the next one in the cycle. In this cycle: Fire melts Metal; Metal cuts Wood; Wood drains from the Earth; Earth absorbs and blocks Water; and Water puts out Fire.

Five Elements — The five elements of Chinese astrology are used in feng shui to indicate the different energies that are around, and in us. The elements are: Fire, Earth, Metal, Water and Wood. They can be arranged in a variety of ways, but the most important arrangements are the *Destructive Cycle* and the *Productive Cycle*.

Form School — The Form School is the original version of feng shui that examines the geography of the landscape to determine the quantity and quality of ch'i available. The perfect site creates an abundance of ch'i, and has an equal amount of yin and yang (flat and hilly).

I Ching — The I Ching, also known as the *Book of Changes,* is the oldest book of China, and probably the world. It was originally devised by Wu of Hsia in 3322 B.C.E. The I Ching was considered so important that when Chin Shih-Huang destroyed all the books in China in 215 B.C.E., the I Ching was spared. This was because he needed the I Ching to rule the country effectively.

Magic Square — A magic square is composed of a series of numbers inside a grid where all the horizontal, vertical and diagonal rows add up to the same number. Magic squares have been popular in China from the time that Wu of Hsia found a three-by-three magic square on the back of a tortoise shell. The pa-kua of feng shui uses this magic square to determine the positions of the eight trigrams.

Pa-kua — The pa-kua is an ancient and powerful symbol of Chinese culture. It is frequently found hanging over the doors of Chinese homes to provide protection. It is eight-sided and usually has either a mirror or the yin-yang symbol in the center. Around this are placed the eight trigrams of the I Ching.

Poison Arrows — See **Shars**

Productive Cycle — The productive cycle is an arrangement of the five elements where each element enhances and encourages the one that follows it in the cycle. In this arrangement: Fire burns and produces Earth; Earth gives birth to Metal; Metal liquefies and symbolically creates Water; Water nurtures and produces Wood; and Wood burns and creates Fire.

Shars — Shars, sometimes known as *poison arrows,* are straight lines or angles of negative energy that give the potential for bad luck or misfortune. A path that leads in a straight line directly to a front door would be considered a shar. An angle created by the roofline or two walls of a neighboring house pointing in your direction is also considered a shar.

Tortoise — A tortoise has been considered a positive omen even before Wu of Hsia found one with a magic square formed in the markings on its shell. In Chinese pre-history people believed that gods lived inside the shells of turtles and tortoises. This is because the shell of the tortoise represents the sky, and consequently heaven, while the stomach represented earth. Consequently, the tortoise is still revered as one of the four spiritual animals of China (along with the dragon, phoenix and unicorn), One favored method of divination at the time of Wu was to heat the shells of tortoises until they cracked, and then interpret the results. Nowadays, the tortoise is considered a symbol of strength, endurance and longevity.

Trigrams — The eight trigrams from the I Ching comprise every possible combination of straight and broken lines that can be created from three lines. The straight lines are called yang lines and represent masculine energy. The broken lines are called yin lines and represent feminine energy.

Wu of Hsia — Wu of Hsia is considered the father of feng shui. He is the first of the five mythical emperors of Chinese pre-history, and is believed to have lived about five thousand years ago. The legend is that a tortoise crawled out of the Yellow River while Wu and his men were performing irrigation work. The markings on the shell created a perfect three-by-three magic square. From this magic square came feng shui, the I Ching, Chinese numerology, and Chinese astrology.

Yin and Yang — Yin and yang are the two opposites that cannot live without the other. They are usually represented as two tadpole-like figures inside a circle. Yin is black, with a white spot inside it, while yang is white with a black spot inside it. Most Westerners recognize this symbol, though they usually have no idea what it means. Yin and yang was never defined, but was demonstrated with lists of the opposites that cannot live without the other. Examples are: night and day, hot and cold, wet and dry, tall and short, front and back, summer and winter, and male and female. Even today the Chinese delight in finding different pairs to represent yin and yang. Yin and yang originally came from the two sides of a mountain. Yin was the cold, shady, North side, while yang represented the warm, sunny, South side. This dualistic view of the universe has played a major role in Chinese culture for thousands of years.

Suggested Reading

Heann-Tatt, Ong. *The Chinese Pakua*. Selangor, Malaysia: Pelanduk Publications, 1991.

Kaptchuk, Ted J. *The Web that has no Weaver*. New York: Congdon and Weed, Inc., 1983.

Marsh, Dr. Peter (ed.). *Eye to Eye: Your Relationships and How They Work*. London: Sidgwick and Jackson Limited, 1988.

Moore, Thomas. *Care of the Soul*. New York: HarperCollins Publishers, Inc., 1992.

Palmer, Martin. *Yin and Yang*. London: Judy Piatkus (Publishers) Limited, 1997.

Saunders, Jeraldine. *Signs of Love*. Los Angeles: Pinnacle Books, Inc., 1977. Republished by Llewellyn Publications, St. Paul, MN, 1998.

Sturt, John and Agnes. *Created for Intimacy*. Guildford, Surrey, UK: Eagle, 1996.

Swan, James A. and Roberta. *Dialogues with the Living Earth.* Wheaton, IL: Quest Books, 1996.

Tsuei, Wei. *Roots of Chinese Culture and Medicine.* Selangor, Malaysia: Pelanduk Publications, 1992.

Webster, Richard. *Feng Shui for Beginners.* St. Paul, MN: Llewellyn Publications, 1997.

Index

FENG SHUI
FOR BEGINNERS

Successful Living by Design

Richard Webster

Not advancing fast enough in your career? Maybe your desk is located in a "negative position." Wish you had a more peaceful family life? Hang a mirror in your dining room and watch what happens. Is money flowing out of your life rather than into it? You may want to look to the construction of your staircase!

For thousands of years, the ancient art of feng shui has helped people harness universal forces and lead lives rich in good health, wealth and happiness. The basic techniques in *Feng Shui for Beginners* are very simple, and you can put them into place immediately in your home and work environments. Gain peace of mind, a quiet confidence, and turn adversity to your advantage with feng shui remedies.

1-56718-803-6, 240 pp., 5 ¼ x 8, photos, softcover $12.95

To order, call 1-800-THE MOON
Prices subject to change without notice

101 FENG SHUI TIPS FOR THE HOME
Richard Webster

For thousand of years, people in the Far East have used feng shui to improve their home and family lives and live in harmony with the earth. Certainly, people who practice feng-shui achieve a deep contentment that is denied most others. They usually do well romantically and financially. Architects around the world are beginning to incorporate the concepts of feng shui into their designs. Even people like Donald Trump freely admit to using feng shui.

Now you can make subtle and inexpensive changes to your home that can literally transform your life. If you're in the market for a house, learn what to look for in room design, single level vs. split level, staircases, front door location and more. If you want to improve upon your existing home, find out how its current design may be creating negative energy, and discover simple ways to remedy the situation without the cost of major renovations or remodeling.

Watch your success and spirits soar when you discover:
- How to evaluate the current feng shui energy in your home
- What to do about negative energy coming from neighbors
- How to use fountains or aquariums to attract money
- The best position for the front door
- How to arrange your living room furniture
- Colors to use and avoid for each member of the family

1-56718-809-5, 192 pp., 5 ¼ x 8, charts   **$9.95**

To order, call 1-800-THE MOON
Prices subject to change without notice

FENG SHUI FOR APARTMENT LIVING
Richard Webster

Don't think that just because you live in an apartment complex, a one-room studio, or a tiny dormitory that you can't benefit from the ancient art of feng shui. You can indeed make subtle changes to your living area that will literally transform your life. Those who practice feng shui are noticing marked improvements in all areas—romantic, financial, career, family, health, even fame. This latest book in Richard Webster's Feng Shui series addresses the special ways that you can improve the harmony and balance in your apartment, at little or no expense.

Learn what to look for when selecting an apartment. Find out where your four positive and four negative locations are, and avoid pointing your bed toward the "disaster" location. Discover the best places for other furniture, and how to remedy negative areas with plants, mirrors, crystals and wind chimes. You will also learn how to conduct a feng shui evaluation for others.

1-56718-794-3, 160 pp., 5 ³/₁₆ x 8, illus., softcover   **$9.95**

To order, call 1-800-THE MOON
Prices subject to change without notice

˙FENG SHUI FOR THE WORKPLACE

Richard Webster

All over the East, business people regularly consult feng shui practitioners because they know it gives them an extra edge for success. Citibank, Chase Asia, the Morgan Bank, Rothschilds and even the Wall Street Journal are just a few examples of leading corporations who use feng shui.

Feng shui is the art of living in harmony with the earth. It's about increasing the flow of "ch'i," in your environment—the universal life force that is found in all living things. Chances are, if you're feeling stuck in your career, your ch'i is also stuck; getting it moving again will benefit you in all areas of your life. Whether you want to increase productivity in your factory, decrease employee turnover in your office, increase sales in your retail store, or bring more customers to your home consulting business, *Feng Shui for the Workplace* offers the tips and solutions for every business scenario. Individual employees can even use this book to decorate their work space for better job satisfaction.

1-56718-808-7, 160 pp., 5 ³/₁₆ x 8, illus., softcover $9.95

To order, call 1-800-THE MOON

SEVEN SECRETS TO SUCCESS
A Story of Hope

Richard Webster

Originally written as a letter from the author to his suicidal friend, this inspiring little book has been photocopied, passed along from person to person, and even appeared on the internet without the author's permission. Now available in book form, this underground classic offers hope to the weary and motivation for us all to let go of the past and follow our dreams.

It is the story of Kevin, who at the age of twenty-eight is on the verge of suicide after the failure of his business and his marriage. Then he meets Todd Melvin, an elderly gentleman with a mysterious past. As their friendship unfolds, Todd teaches Kevin seven secrets—secrets that can give you the power to turn your life around, begin anew, and reap success beyond your wildest dreams.

1-56718-797-8, 144 pp., 5 ³⁄₁₆ x 8, softcover   **$6.95**

AURA READING
FOR BEGINNERS
Richard Webster

When you lose your temper, don't be surprised if a dirty red haze suddenly appears around you. If you do something magnanimous, your aura will expand. Now you can learn to see the energy that emanates off yourself and other people through the proven methods taught by Richard Webster in his psychic training classes.

Learn to feel the aura, see the colors in it, and interpret what those colors mean. Explore the chakra system, and how to restore balance to chakras that are over- or under-stimulated. Then you can begin to imprint your desires into your aura to attract what you want in your life.

These proven methods for seeing the aura will help you:

- Interpret the meanings of colors in the aura
- Find a career that is best suited for you
- Relate better to the people you meet and deal with
- Enjoy excellent health
- Discover areas of your life that you need to work on
- Imprint what you want in your future into your aura
- Make aura portraits with pastels or colored pencils
- Change the state of your aura and stimulate specific chakras through music, crystals, color

1-56718-798-6, 208 pp., 5 ³/₁₆ x 8, illus.   **$7.95**

ASTRAL TRAVEL
FOR BEGINNERS
Richard Webster

Astral projection, or the out-of-body travel, is a completely natural experience. You have already astral traveled thousands of times in your sleep, you just don't remember it when you wake up. Now, you can learn how to leave your body at will, be fully conscious of the experience, and remember it when you return.

The exercises in this book are carefully graded to take you step-by-step through an actual out-of-body experience. Once you have accomplished this, it becomes easier and easier to leave your body. That's why the emphasis in this book is on your first astral travel.

The ability to astral travel can change your life. You will have the freedom to go anywhere and do anything. You can explore new worlds, go back and forth through time, make new friends and even find a lover on the astral planes. Most importantly, you will find that you no longer fear death as you discover that you are indeed a spiritual being independent of your physical body.

By the time you have finished the exercises in this book you will be able to leave your body and explore the astral realms with confidence and total safety:

- Instantly visit any place in the world that you desire

- Transport yourself back or forward through time

- Lose all fear of death

- Find love on the astral plane

- Practice remote viewing without leaving your body

1-56718-796-X, 256 pp., 5 ³/₁₆ x 8   **$9.95**

To order, call 1-800-THE MOON
Prices subject to change without notice

SPIRIT GUIDES & ANGEL GUARDIANS
Contact Your Invisible Helpers

Richard Webster

They come to our aid when we least expect it, and they disappear as soon as their work is done. Invisible helpers are available to all of us; in fact, we all regularly receive messages from our guardian angels and spirit guides but usually fail to recognize them. This book will help you to realize when this occurs. And when you carry out the exercises provided, you will be able to communicate freely with both your guardian angels and spirit guides.

You will see your spiritual and personal growth take a huge leap forward as soon as you welcome your angels and guides into your life. This book contains numerous case studies that show how angels have touched the lives of others, just like yourself. Experience more fun, happiness and fulfillment than ever before. Other people will also notice the difference as you become calmer, more relaxed and more loving than ever before.

- Invoke the Archangels for help in achieving your goals
- Discover the different ways your guardian angel speaks to you
- Create your own guardian angel from within
- Enhance your creativity by calling on angelic assistance
- Find your life's purpose through your guardian angel
- Use time-tested methods to contact your spirit guides
- Use your spirit guides to help you release negative emotions
- Call on specific guides for nurturing, support, fun, motivation, wisdom

ISBN: 1-56718-795-1, 368 pp., 5 3/16 x 8   **$9.95**

CHINESE
NUMEROLOGY
Richard Webster

This book goes back to the very beginnings of numerology, to a time when people thought gods lived in turtle shells, and when the discovery of a tortoise containing a perfect magic square in its markings was an event of national importance. *Chinese Numerology* teaches the original system of numerology which is still practiced throughout the East, and from which Chinese astrology, feng-shui and the I Ching were all derived.

Chinese numerology as presented here is the quickest and easiest method of character analysis ever devised. Early into the book, you will be able to build a complete picture of a person just as soon as you know his or her birthdate. By the end of the book, you will be able to erect and interpret numerology charts in three different ways. With this knowledge, you will know more about yourself and the motivations of others. You'll also know when to move ahead and when to hold back in different areas of your life.

Includes solar-lunar conversion tables to the year 2000.

1-56718-804-4, 260 pp., 7 x 10　　　　　　　　　**$12.95**

NUMEROLOGY
MAGIC
Richard Webster

Based upon the ancient Eastern numerology system in use for more than 4,000 years, *Numerology Magic* explores the magical "yantras"—numbered squares as individual and meaningful as your astrological birth chart. It's easy to gain valuable insights into your motivations, character, and potentials with Richard Webster's step-by-step instructions.

Long deemed to possess great magical properties, yantra number squares are also incredibly powerful energy channels for attracting your sincerest desires. You can use your personal yantra as a potent talisman to transform undesirable circumstances, attract money, help you accomplish life goals, and even bind lovers closer together.

1-56718-813-3, 192 pp., 5 ³⁄₁₆ x 8, illus.   **$7.95**

100 DAYS TO BETTER HEALTH, GOOD SEX & LONG LIFE
A Guide to Taoist Yoga & Chi Kung

Eric Steven Yudelove

Mankind has always sought ways to achieve better health and increased longevity. To these ends, the Taoists of China achieved great success; living 100 years or more was quite common. Now, Eric Yudelove's latest book presents a complete course in Taoist health, sexual rejuvenation and longevity practices. These practices are not religious, but they are often quite different from what we are used to. And this is the first time that much of this knowledge is available to Western readers.

The curriculum is presented in 14 weekly lessons (100 days) that take 15 minutes a day. Each week you will learn exercises for the Three Treasures of Taoism: Chi, Jing and Shen—or breath, body and mind. *100 Days...* introduces you to the powerful Chi Kung, the Six Healing Sounds, Baduanjin, self massage, sexual kung fu, the inner smile, opening the golden flower and much more.

1-56718-833-8, 320 pp., 7 x 10, illus., softcover $17.95